**This Large Print Book carries the
Seal of Approval of N.A.V.H.**

Shirley Jones

Shirley Jones

—A Memoir—

Shirley Jones
with Wendy Leigh

CENTER POINT LARGE PRINT
THORNDIKE, MAINE

This Center Point Large Print edition is published in the year 2013 by arrangement with Gallery Books, a division of Simon & Schuster, Inc.

The text of this Large Print edition is unabridged. In other aspects, this book may vary from the original edition. Printed in the United States of America on permanent paper. Set in 16-point Times New Roman type.

ISBN: 978-1-61173-868-1

Library of Congress Cataloging-in-Publication Data

Jones, Shirley, 1934 March 31–
   Shirley Jones : a memoir / Shirley Jones. — Center Point Large Print edition.
   pages ; cm.
   ISBN 978-1-61173-868-1 (library binding : alk. paper)
   1. Jones, Shirley, 1934 March 31–
      2. Actresses—United States—Biography.
      3.Women singers—United States—Biography.
      4. Large type books. I. Title.
PN2287.J63A3 2013b
791.4302'8092—dc23
   [B]
                                                          2013017082

To my glorious father,
who loved me as I was
and left me far too early

CONTENTS

INTRODUCTION

For those of you who remember me as the innocent, blond, blue-eyed ingénue of *Oklahoma!* and *Carousel* and *The Music Man*, the real-life, everyday me is far removed from the characters of Laurey, Julie, and Marian the librarian. While I was proud to sing great American standards such as "People Will Say We're in Love," "If I Loved You," and "Till There Was You" for the very first time on-screen, I have never myself been that innocent or ever been that kind of an ingénue.

Similarly, for those of you who remember me as Mrs. Partridge of *The Partridge Family*, while I adored being a real-life mother to my four boys (Shaun, Patrick, Ryan, and David, who is my stepson), I am nowhere near as breezy and uncomplicated as Mrs. Partridge. And I'm not a spoiled Hollywood movie star or a jaded TV icon, either.

Deep down I am a small-town girl from Smithton, Pennsylvania, who made movies with such actors as Marlon Brando, Rod Steiger, Henry Fonda, James Cagney, Burt Lancaster, Glenn

Ford, David Niven, Rossano Brazzi, and Pat Boone. I appeared on TV with my stepson, David Cassidy, and the rest of the wonderful cast of *The Partridge Family*, but also with Farrah Fawcett, Richard Pryor, Jerry Lewis, and Dean Martin. I partied with Richard Burton, Elizabeth Taylor, and Joan Collins; I performed for President Eisenhower, President Johnson, President Ford, President Reagan, and the first President Bush; and I rubbed shoulders with Sammy Davis Jr., Judy Garland, Frank Sinatra, Orson Welles, Warren Beatty, George C. Scott, and Cary Grant. And I was married twice: first to the ultimate lothario, Tony Award–winning star Jack Cassidy, and then to the zany actor/producer Marty Ingels, who is my current husband. Along the way, I won an Academy Award as well.

But deep down I remain that small-town girl from Smithton, Pennsylvania, and in the dead of the night, in my secret soul, I still sometimes wish I had taken a different path and never gone into show business, but followed my dreams and become a veterinarian instead.

In this memoir you are going to meet the real, flesh-and-blood Shirley Jones, not just the movie star or Mrs. Partridge. While my life may, on the surface, seem to be full of glitter and glamour, from the inside looking out that is far from the whole.

In my private life, I've had struggles, dilemmas,

and tragedies—some of the same struggles, dilemmas, and tragedies that many other women of my generation have had to cope with: the early death of a parent, marriage to a rampantly unfaithful first husband, watching helplessly while a child battled a drug habit, trying to make peace between a second husband and children from a previous marriage, and all the usual challenges in growing old.

And then there is my sexuality, when I was in my prime and now that I am on the threshold of my eighties. I plan to tell the truth about that aspect of my life, and to rip away the seven veils and reveal every facet of Shirley Jones, however shocking that may be to you or Mrs. Partridge or Marian the librarian.

So bring out the smelling salts, hang on to your hats, and get ready for the surprise of your lives!

ONE

A Beautiful Morning

Although I was named Shirley after the saccharine child star Shirley Temple, I've always been far more full of spice than of sugar.

As a baby, instead of cooing away softly and then serenely sleeping all day in my crib, I screamed and screamed at the top of my voice until I got attention. My favorite pastime was chewing on my crib because I seemed to like the taste of varnish so much. I chewed so hard, and with such great determination, that chew marks were left all over the wooden rails of my crib.

I was sturdy, adventurous, and unafraid. When I was four years old, and playing in the family-owned Jones brewery, my grandfather promised me jelly beans if I drank some beer. I jumped at the opportunity, tried the beer, and hated it.

But I loved the brewery, and everything about it, primarily because it was my haven, my second home. My father, Paul Jones, and his brothers ran the Smithton, Pennsylvania, brewery, and from the time when I was three years old and we moved from Charleroi, Pennsylvania, where I was born, I spent much of my childhood there, playing hide-and-seek among the beer vats and the ice lockers, while my father's employees all held their breath, terrified that I would accidentally lock myself in a freezer and emerge as a pint-size ice sculpture!

The Jones Brewing Company employed at least half of Smithton (population only 800), and it was started by my grandfather William B. Jones, who hailed from Wales. He immigrated to Pennsylvania, became a coal miner, worked him-self to the bone, and saved enough money to buy a corner building in the little town of Smithton, a Norman Rockwell painting in living color. Then he converted that building into a small hotel with six rooms and called it the Jones Hotel. He was the bartender, and my grand-mother Lulu did every-thing else necessary to make the hotel run smoothly.

The official story, the one that I grew up knowing by heart, was that the hotel was so successful my grandfather bought a building on a beautiful site on the Youghiogheny River, which flowed through Smithton, joined the Monongahela River, and then ran right into Pittsburgh, twenty-one miles away. In 1907, in that riverside building, he founded the Jones Brewing Company.

The unofficial story, one that I heard years later, was that William B. Jones, my grandfather, actually won the brewery in a poker game!

According to that tale, the brewery had originally been based in Sutersville, Pennsylvania, and manufactured Eureka beer. After my grandfather won the brewery in 1907, he renamed it the Jones Brewing Company and moved it to Smithton.

Whatever the truth, I'm sure of one thing, the origin of the name of Jones brewery's most beloved beer. According to family lore, one of my grandfather's earliest customers was an African-American man who regularly visited the brewery along with his bulldog, Stoney.

My grandfather grew to love that dog so much that after the dog died, he declared, "From now on, my name is Stoney Jones." And he named the beer he brewed Stoney's beer after the dog he loved so much.

Since then, the Jones Brewing Company, Stoney's beer, and Stoney's Light beer have been featured in the movie *Striking Distance*, starring Bruce Willis, and in the TV shows *Northern Exposure* and *My Name Is Earl*.

Although I never knew my grandfather well, I inherited his love of animals and, as a child, raised mice, birds, squirrels, and had no fear of snakes or spiders. No fear whatsoever. In fact, my biggest ambition was to become a vet and look after animals of all types and sizes. Then, fate took a hand and I became something quite different.

My grandfather died of diabetes aged only fifty-six, after having his leg amputated, rumor had it, because he drank too much beer. Sometime before he died, he tried to reverse his diabetes by instructing that Stoney's beer be manufactured without sugar. Sadly, that didn't help, and he died anyway. Nonetheless, even today, Stoney's beer is still manufactured without sugar or preservatives.

After my grandfather's untimely death, my formidable grandmother Lulu inherited the Jones brewery, and my father and his brothers ran it for her.

Despite his responsibilities, my father was a relaxed, generous, and happy man, with a heart of gold. From the first, he was the love of my life. When I was in the crib and screamed until it felt as if my lungs would burst, he would immediately rush into my nursery at top speed, lift me high in his strong, muscular arms, then place me on his barrel chest, whereupon I would promptly fall into a deep, contented sleep.

In contrast, my mother never came to my rescue when I screamed. She just let me go on screaming and screaming. She was much too busy running our home, or entertaining guests. But while my father was always the life and soul of the party, my mother was not.

Her name was Marjorie, and she was born Williams, of English descent. Her father was a telephone lineman, she had two sisters, and when she met my father, she fell in love with him at first sight.

That love was to last a lifetime, but from as far back as I can remember, my mother continually appeared to be suffering from a deep and abiding disappointment. As I grew older and got to know my mother better, it became eminently clear to me that when she married my father, of the Jones Brewing Company, she had expected far more out of life and, forever afterward, desperately longed to get out of Smithton and move into the big city.

But despite my mother's unfulfilled expectations, she loved my father unconditionally and adored him unreservedly. I never saw her fight with him, and even though he sometimes came home drunk, I never saw her get angry with him. Drunk as he was, she would undress him, get him ready for bed, and take care of him without a word of complaint. Looking back through the years, I realize that because from the time when I was a small child I watched my mother display such love and tolerance toward my father, her example unconsciously formed my own attitude toward men, in general, and to my first and second husbands, in particular.

My father was away from home a great deal, traveling from Pittsburgh-area saloon to saloon, selling Stoney's beer. Now and again, to my joy and excitement, he would scoop me up and take me with him on his travels. Together, we would drive through the countryside in his gray Chevy, talking away, drinking in the beauty of the Pennsylvania countryside.

Our route always took us over one particular bridge across the Youghiogheny River, through farmland where cattle and horses peacefully grazed. My father would invariably stop the car and just sit there, gazing at the animals. "They are so beautiful, Shirley," he would say, "so beautiful." Witnessing my father's deep reverence for animals and for nature bequeathed to me an enduring love for animals and nature, as well.

Once we arrived at a saloon, he would sell cases of Stoney's beer to the saloon owner, then go up to the bar, put up a sign, BUY STONEY'S BEER, and place beers for everyone at the bar, while I played on the pinball machine to my heart's content.

I couldn't help noticing that wherever we went, women were all over my father. He was such a handsome man. Years later, I once asked him if he had ever cheated on my mother, and he smiled and said, "I just played at it. I patted a few asses now and again, but I didn't do more than that." And I believed him.

He was kind and loving, perhaps because he was the youngest son and had grown up very loved by his mother, Lulu, my grandmother.

After my grandfather died, my grandmother became the matriarch of the family. My mother and father and I lived with her in a fourteen-room brick house on the corner of Second Street in

Smithton. The house had a huge front porch, which ran half the length of the street and looked warm and welcoming.

My mother and father and I had seven rooms in the house, my grandmother had the rest, and a door led between my grandmother's kitchen and ours. Every morning, I would wake up and run to have tea and toast with my grandma in her kitchen.

She was the boss lady who owned the brewery, handed out paychecks, and gave a big Christmas party every year for her family and employees at Sweeney's Restaurant and Lounge on Route 51 in Belle Vernon. She was a great role model, a tough lady who had to fight to stay on top in a man's world.

My world, in contrast, was safe and secure. As an only child, I had my own room, with my own little desk in one corner, a blackboard in another, and all the toys I wanted. I had a tricycle I loved, every paper doll known to man, and countless real dolls.

I adored my dolls, one in particular named Carol, who had a huge china head, big blue eyes, and a body bigger than the average baby's. She was so startlingly lifelike that one time I even dressed her in the hat and dress that my mother took me home from the hospital in and painted her nails. Now that same doll belongs to my granddaughter Megan, my youngest son Ryan's child, and she loves Carol as much as I did all those decades ago.

• • •

Smithton was a classic all-American small town, like River City in *The Music Man*, made up of only four streets, and my childhood there was idyllic. The biggest house in the town belonged to Dr. Post and stood on top of the hill at the end of Fourth Street.

All us kids always looked up at Dr. Post's house—a country-style home with white shutters, a lot of land, and a big fence around it—and dreamed of one day living in such an imposing and impressive mansion ourselves.

Meanwhile, as we all waited to grow up, we relished our childhood in Smithton. Our world was small, self-contained, innocent, and ideal. Smithton was so tiny that the town had no policemen, only a sheriff, and there was just one movie theater, the Smithton Movie House, which played movies only on the weekend.

Smithton boasted just one grocery store, a drugstore, and a little variety store, which sold toys and clothes and candy. When I was six, overcome by an uncharacteristic surge of greed, I grabbed a stick of bubble gum from the store, slipped it into my pocket, and skipped home with it. When my mother saw me open the bubble-gum packet, she asked where I got the money to buy bubble gum for myself, and I confessed that I had just snatched it from the store. Outraged, she immediately insisted that I return it to the store right away. So I trudged over there, declared to the shocked owner, "I took your bubble gum," and threw it right back at him.

Afterward, my mother sent me up to my room in disgrace and told me to stay there until she gave me permission to come out. So I stomped upstairs into my bedroom, slammed the door, then tore the linens off the bed, the drapes off the windows, swept everything off the dresser, and dragged it all out into the middle of the room.

When my mother eventually came upstairs and yelled through the door that I could come out now, I yelled back defiantly, "Why don't you come in and look at my room?"

She did, drank in all the chaos I had created, and ordered me to put everything back in its place again. Naturally, I couldn't do that on my own, so I got one of my friends to help me instead. I didn't feel guilty about what I had done, either. I was already a little hell-raiser, and proud of it.

Another quintessential story from my child-hood as Shirley, the precocious little rebel: When I was five years old, my mother took me to the dentist. After examining my teeth, the dentist announced that I had to have a tooth pulled.

I shook my head and stamped my feet, but to no avail. An appointment was made for the dreaded extraction of my errant tooth.

When the morning of the appointment dawned, my mother and father accompanied me to the dentist, along with my favorite aunt, my mother's sister, Aunt Ina.

In the car, I kept yelling that I wasn't going to have my tooth pulled, no way, no how.

My mother, to her credit, was kind and patient and kept reassuring me, "Now, sweetheart, it's not going to hurt. Your aunt Ina's here, your daddy's here, I'm here. Everything is going to be all right."

I should have believed her, but being the child that I was, by the time we all climbed to the top of the stairs in the dentist's building and stood outside his office door, I plainly did not. So I pulled away from my family and ran downstairs again.

All of them, my mother, my father, and Aunt Ina stood at the top of the stairs, begging me to come back.

I just kept shaking my head and stayed put at the bottom of the stairs, and out of reach.

Then Aunt Ina hit on a winning formula: "Listen, sweetheart, if you come up the stairs again, I'll buy you a pony."

Won over by her promise, I looked at my mother first, then at my father, and both of them nodded encouragingly.

"Come up, sweetheart, I'll hold your hand and nothing's going to hurt you, I promise," Aunt Ina said.

Mollified, I ran upstairs, and my mother, my father, and Aunt Ina, all grabbed me and put me in the dentist's chair. Within moments, the dentist had injected me with anesthetic, then yanked out my tooth.

"But where's my pony? Where's my pony?" I cried, when I woke up.

I looked questioningly at my mother, my father, and Aunt Ina. None of them met my gaze.

The dentist exchanged glances with my father, then shrugged.

The writing was on the wall.

I stuck my face straight into the dentist's and yelled, "I'm not getting a pony. And you're a big shit!"

I don't know where or how I learned that particular word, but I was on the right track, really. Because over the next few months, however often I asked my mother, my father, or Aunt Ina where my pony was, however much I begged and cajoled, I always got the same answer: "It's coming soon."

Not surprisingly, my pony never did materialize, and I was angry with Aunt Ina, with my parents, and with the dentist. They had all lied to me, and I didn't like it at all. Which is probably partly why I became even more of a rebel. The other reason, I guess, was that I was just born that way.

I was willful, stubborn, and determined to do exactly what I wanted to do when I wanted to do it. I was unable to follow rules, or to act in the way in which a well-bred young lady was supposed to act. From as far back as I can remember, everyone who knew me agreed that I was already my own person.

The dentist incident caused me to loose trust in adults, but I think yet another reason for my tendency to rebel at every turn and to be a tomboy so early on was because I knew that my father had always wanted a son, and because I loved him so much, I wanted to please him.

So I yearned to be a boy and to do everything that boys did, only better. I refused to wear dresses and did whatever I could to prove that I was as tough as any boy and could do exactly the same things as boys could, only better.

After my father taught me sports and took me to all the Pirates games, I became a great baseball and softball and basketball player and, down the line, became head majorette in high school.

My father was delighted by my sporting prowess and made sure that I knew it, praising me at every turn. My mother, however, was not amused that I wasn't evolving into a nice, well-brought-up, little Shirley Temple–type young lady. Practically every morning, after I refused to wear a dress to school, or to comb my hair, my mother paddled me with whatever she could lay her hands on, from a hairbrush to a spatula. If I came home covered in mud or threw my clothes all over the floor, in the evening my mother paddled me again.

In retrospect, I don't blame her, because I just flatly refused to take orders. The moment she—or anyone else—told me to do anything, I did exactly the opposite.

When I wasn't rebelling against authority directly, I was causing trouble in other ways. One Sunday night at around seven o'clock, when I was nine years old and hanging out with my best friend, Red, and my cousin Joanne, I pressed the town's fire alarm, just to see what would happen. The second I did it, sirens blared, and the Smithton Volunteer Fire Department truck pulled up outside the café where we were hanging out.

Red and Joanne and I ran away as fast as we could, but someone ratted on us. Before we could make our getaway, we were hauled in front of the sheriff, who read us the riot act, in front of our parents, who had been called down to witness our rebuke and disgrace. Terrified, I mustered up the courage to ask the sheriff if we were facing jail. Jail, he told me gravely, was a real possibility, reform school at the very least.

Red, Joanne, and I were white with terror. Luckily for us, though, the sheriff took pity on us and relented. We were too young to go to jail, he announced, and instead he presented each of us with a piece of paper, ordering us to check in with him once a month for the entire year, without fail. We did and thanked our lucky stars that we got off so easily.

Apart from my sporadic bursts of rebellion, life in Smithton had a leisurely rhythm to it, a serenity in common with that of many American small towns. Every Sunday, my mother would make a big dinner at our house. She was a good cook, and her signature recipe was City Chicken—chicken, beef, and veal meatballs on a skewer, coated in bread crumbs, then put in the oven with vegetables.

Usually my grandmother ate with us, and so did my aunts, and during dinner and afterward we would all sit around talking local talk—about the brewery, what Mrs. so-and-so did today, what the grocery man said—the kind of conversation that only goes on in small towns all over America. If anything out of turn happened to disturb the routine of the town, that became a big deal indeed.

Animals were always the biggest deal in my life. Many times when my father came home late at night after being out all day on the road selling beer—often starting at eight and getting back home to us at three in the morning—to my delight he would bring home a puppy or a kitten as a gift for me.

Best of all, when I was very young, he brought home a dalmatian puppy, whom I instantly named Spot. I was devoted to Spot; he swiftly became my chief confidant, and I told him my deepest secrets constantly, so I was devastated when— around my tenth birthday—I came home from school one day to find that Spot had disappeared.

Distraught, I ran to my mother and demanded to know where Spot was.

My mother shrugged her shoulders. "I don't know. Last thing I saw, he went over to visit your grandmother."

I ran over to my grandmother's part of the house and begged her to tell me where Spot was.

All my grandmother would say was "Oh, sweetheart, I'm so sorry. I gave Spot a piece of cheese and he ran away because he didn't like it."

Young as I was, I didn't believe her. Particularly when I remembered that, the day before, Spot had raced out into her garden and dug up her cherished rhubarb plants. I drew my own conclusions, and I was not happy. For a while, my feelings toward my grandmother altered radically.

Instead of mourning Spot for too long, though, I drowned my sorrows in playing with my other pet, a little terrier I called Snoopy, who was no bigger than a Chihuahua.

Then there was school, which I adored. Our school housed two grades in a single room and went up to eighth grade; then you went on to high school.

From third grade on, my best friend was Red, who is still my best friend today. I lived at one end of the town, and she lived six blocks away from me at the other. Red and I were always together, and when the boys came up to me and yelled,

"Who do you think you are?" (because my family owned the Jones brewery), or threw mud at me, Red would be right there, sticking by me.

Not that I needed any support, really. I was always a big fighter and would think nothing of battling the boys until my nose was bloody and my hair torn out in shreds. I didn't care. I just wanted to win, and I usually did.

Part of the problem, I think, is that a few of the boys thought I was some kind of princess—the heiress to the Jones Brewing Company—and spoiled. But that wasn't true. I wasn't in the least bit spoiled. Although I was an only child, I never felt that I was given more than anyone else. My friends were never jealous of me or competitive with me or treated me as if I were in any way different from them. I was one of them and always would be. I still have friends whom I first met when we were in the third grade together.

But while I loved school, I didn't love what awaited me when I got home from school, the paddling that my mother invariably gave me. At times, it seemed to me as if I got daily paddlings, and maybe I did.

I was so strong, so determined; I wanted what I wanted, and no one could divert me from it. I hated authority, and I was set on getting my way, come hell or high water. So I got paddled, over and over.

To me it seemed that my mother thought that

everything I did was wrong—and she punished me accordingly.

I was constantly shut up in my room, banned from going out with my friends, and paddled. I took my punishment stoically, rarely cried, and in a way the paddlings became part of my life. Then one day, I just had enough.

I was nine years old and, after a particularly heavy paddling (I'd moved the blackboard from one wall to another in my room, had undone my ponytail, or whatever other transgression had made my mother mad), sat on the landing with my dalmatian, Spot (who hadn't yet vandalized my grandmother's garden and been spirited away by her), next to me. I was sore and sad. The only one around to comfort me was Spot.

So I put my arms around him, held him close, gazed deep into his eyes, and started confiding in him. "Spot, I don't know what I'm gonna do. It's just not working out for me. I guess I've got to change my ways," I said ruefully.

Spot looked up at me and wagged his tail.

The next morning, just before school, for the first time in my life I put on a dress. I remember that dress to this day: peach-colored taffeta with puffed sleeves.

As I came downstairs into the kitchen, my mother was making breakfast and had her back to me. My aunt Ina, however, did not.

"Look at that, Marge, Shirley's wearing a

dress! Isn't that exactly what you wanted?"

My mother spun around, looked me up and down, and smiled radiantly. "Well, Shirley, how nice you look! How lovely you look! Isn't that wonderful? I'm so proud of you!"

I felt great. *I guess I've got to start pleasing my mother more,* I said to myself.

And that's what I did for quite a few years, until I hit my early teens and all hell broke loose.

Until then, I was basically a good girl, who, when she wasn't playing the tomboy and getting dirty, loved playing with her dolls. Dolls were now things of the past for me. Instead, I was obsessed with movies and movie stars. I plastered the walls of my bedroom with pictures of my idols: Fred Astaire, Judy Garland, Lana Turner, Howard Duff, and—my all-time favorite—Burt Lancaster. If you had told me then that one day I would meet him and make a movie with him— *Elmer Gantry*—I wouldn't have believed you in a billion years.

I adored movies and movie stars and longed to look like one. When I was nine years old, I wore lipstick for the first time. I wore full makeup a year later. I cut my hair before all my friends did, and I was the first girl in town to wear a strapless dress to the prom.

A rebel in everything, in my early teens I tried sloe gin and got so sick that my friend Red had to put me in the shower so that my parents wouldn't smell it on my breath when they came home.

I was wild, willful, and independent, and only three elements in my young life served to make me toe the line to some degree.

The first was my father, for whom I could do no wrong. I would have died if I had disappointed him, and that sentiment kept me on the straight and narrow.

Then there was my love for animals, and for nature, both of which tamed my unruly personality.

Last but not least was the other great love of my life: singing.

When I was four years old, Aunt Ina and I were playing on the swings together. Out of the blue, she asked me if I knew how to sing "God Bless America."

Without any hesitation, I launched into "God Bless America," both word-perfect and pitch-perfect, and Aunt Ina practically fell off the swing in shock.

Within moments she was yelling at my mother, "Marge, have you heard your daughter sing?"

My mother rushed out into the yard, and Aunt Ina asked me to sing "God Bless America" again. For the first time in my four years, I was an obliging child and, on cue, sang another chorus of "God Bless America." My mother was ecstatic.

From that moment on, she would always encourage me in my singing and would years later always write the lyrics of the songs I sang on three-by-five cue cards, so that I would never forget them.

To me, my aunt and my mother seemed to be praising me for something that I took for granted. I didn't understand what all the fuss was about. I thought all children could sing like me, and as easily.

At my mother's and my aunt's behest, from then on I sang at all our family functions, in particular at my grandmother's end-of-summer family party, which she held at Sweeney's Restaurant and Lounge, where we had all our big celebrations.

Most of the time, young as I was, I sang my favorite song, "Frankie and Johnny," about the gal who "shot her lover down." I sang it at one Christmas party and shocked my family to the core. When my choice of song was more suitable for a child of my age, sometimes my cousins joined in, and though I would try not to, I invariably drowned them out.

At six, I was the youngest member of the Universalist Church Choir, and I knew all the hymns by heart. Everyone said that I had a magnificent voice, but I was never vain or conceited about my singing talent. I believed—and still do believe—that my voice was a gift from God.

I loved singing, and I loved my mother's reaction to my singing. My voice, she said, was "wonderful," and I basked in the warm glow of her praise.

But that didn't mean that I was suddenly transformed into an obedient, well-behaved child. After my mother suggested that I take piano lessons, and I had five, I flatly refused to take any more because I hated the lessons, and besides, I just didn't like playing the piano.

But nothing would stop me from singing and glorying it. In the summer of 1946, when I was twelve, my parents sent me to camp on Lake Erie. Over eight weeks, I spent every evening with the other kids, sitting around the fireplace, roasting hot dogs and singing song after song, popular songs, patriotic songs, and religious songs— "The Star-Spangled Banner," "The Lord's Prayer." For the first time in my life I could sing my heart out, and I adored every minute of it.

Not only that, I had an angel watching over me, my camp counselor, Peggy Demler, who had platinum hair down to her shoulders and played Broadway show tunes on the piano as if she were born to do so. From the first, she made no bones about how she considered my voice to be God-given and special.

Peggy loved to play the piano while I sang and gave me guidance on how to enhance my singing voice. When the summer ended, Peggy called my mother and told her that I had an extreme talent and that I ought to have singing lessons.

Moreover, Phyllis Decker Rocker, my singing teacher at South Huntingdon High School, also believed I was already a talented singer and encouraged me to pursue singing as my career. Luckily for me, my mother listened to Peggy Demler and Phyllis Decker Rocker and enrolled me with singing teacher Ralph Lewando, who was the music critic for the *Pittsburgh Press* and who, along with his wife, Olga, was famous as being the top voice coach in Pennsylvania.

My father drove me to and from Pittsburgh once a week for my lessons there, an added bonus being I would be alone with my beloved father during the journey. He was delighted that I was having singing lessons, predicted that my name would one day be up in lights, and always treated me as if I were the princess of the world.

However, my singing teacher, Ralph Lewando, was quite another story. Although he was enchanted by my voice from the very first time I sang for him, he had firm ideas about my future and exactly where he thought my singing talent should lead me.

After I'd sung just a few notes, he stopped me in midsong and announced that I was a born opera singer—a coloratura soprano—no question about it. That was my talent, my gift, my mission in life, he decreed; my God-given vocation was clear.

Much as I respected Ralph Lewando, I didn't agree with him. I didn't want to be an opera singer. So I plucked up the courage to tell the august Mr. Lewando that actually I wanted to sing musical comedy as well as opera. He was taken aback, and although he reluctantly agreed to allow me to sing the odd Broadway tune now and again, he made it clear that he thought singing show tunes was harmful to my voice. I didn't argue with him. I just listened to his instructions, studied hard, practiced religiously, and sang aria after aria, but deep down, I knew that however beautiful the arias were, my heart still belonged to the Broadway musical.

Peggy Demler, my camp counselor at Lake Erie, had played Broadway songs to me so enchantingly, and my father often took me to see musicals when Broadway touring companies played Pittsburgh. My passion for Broadway and the Broadway musical began early in my life. Every summer from as far back as I could remember, my parents and I drove from Pittsburgh to New York and spent a week there, the highlight of which was seeing a Broadway show together.

The very first was *Oklahoma!*

TWO

A Beautiful Day

From as far back as I can remember, my husband Marty has always marveled at my Academy Award acceptance speech in which I said, "This is the happiest day of my career."

"Not your life?" he always exclaims, scratching his head.

"Definitely not" is always my answer.

The plain and simple truth, you see, is that my career has never been my life, and vice versa.

Even in my early teens, when I was singing at Lions Club events, local amateur events, and at clubs in and around the Pittsburgh and being complimented by all and sundry for my singing talent, much as I loved singing, I had other, equally important things on my mind.

My love for animals, of course. And more and more, my passion for boys. One in particular, a boy named Lou Malone. I first became aware of Lou when he was fifteen; I was twelve. He lived across the road from me. A Smithton boy to his fingertips, Lou was tall, blond, with dazzling blue eyes, and made the heart of every girl in town beat much faster. I was no exception.

After Lou and I took a stroll around the neighborhood one night, we ended up in front of my house, as usual. Only this time, I leaned against the old oak tree and Lou kissed me. As he did, I was overcome with a mixture of passion and revulsion.

Chivalrous and polite, Lou quickly said good-night and left me standing there in the moonlight. Confused, and torn between my burgeoning desire and my revulsion, feeling momentarily bereft, I stripped a piece of bark off the old oak tree and sequestered it inside my little memory box as a souvenir.

I was given that box at my third-birthday party and right away hid an artificial flower and a dog's collar, both presents from my friends, inside the box. In time, more of my childish souvenirs joined those first two in my memory box, but this, the bark from the oak tree under which Lou had given me my first kiss, was the most evocative.

The night of my first kiss, I dallied outside, under the oak tree, long after he left. Partly because I felt as if I were floating high above myself, partly because I was afraid that if I went back inside the house straightaway, my mother would sense just by looking at me that Lou Malone had kissed me, and she would get mad at me. Even though Lou was a straight-A student, a football star, and went to a local high school, he was a Catholic, and I knew my mother wouldn't be happy about that.

Fortunately, Red was dating Lou's best friend, which seemed to make it all right when the four of us went to the movies together on one special Saturday night. After a few more Saturday-night double dates like that, my mother grudgingly accepted that Lou and I were an item for keeps.

By the time I was fifteen, Lou became a West Point cadet, and I only had eyes for him. I was his girlfriend, and everyone in Smithton knew it. It probably seemed to them that our marrying one day was a foregone conclusion.

Lou was at the top of his class, and in his plebe year he invited me to West Point for the weekend and presented me with his pin. He was in love with me, he said, and he wanted us to be together for the rest of our lives.

Although Lou's declaration did not come as a surprise to me, I still went very quiet, didn't commit to anything, and on the way home to Smithton gave my future a great deal of thought. I remember ultimately concluding with regret that although Lou was a wonderful man and would become a wonderful doctor when he graduated, being married to him was not the life for me. I wanted more.

I wanted to be in show business because I could sing, to go to college, to star on Broadway, and not to be a wife. Besides, I'd already met another man. . . .

Lou was stable and strong and conventional, but young as I was, I knew that those qualities did not set me on fire. I wanted something else. I wanted adventure. And adventure I would later get in my marriages, both to Jack Cassidy and to Marty Ingels. But even way back then, when I was still in my early teens, I knew without a shadow of a doubt that I wanted a challenge, an unconventional man. And, boy, did I find him!

Bill Boninni was not a Smithton boy. Far from it. He was Italian, with thick, black, curly hair; he wasn't tall; he drove a red Cadillac convertible; and his wealthy father owned a restaurant in Pittsburgh. More important to me than any of that, he had a sense of humor just like my father had, and sadly, when all was said and done, Lou didn't have one at all.

I was just sixteen years old on the day when Bill and I first met. He was nineteen years old. My friend Red and I were sunbathing on the beach by Conneaut Lake, where my aunt had a cabin, and Bill and a friend, Roy, came over and introduced themselves to us.

Soon the four of us were speeding along in Bill's Caddy, bound for a nearby restaurant. He was so charming, so citified, so different from all the Smithton boys I knew, that when he asked if he could see me again, I agreed.

Only when he pulled up in front of my house in his red Cadillac convertible a couple of days later did word of my new gentleman caller spread all over Smithton. Fortunately, Lou was away at West Point and the news did not reach him at that early stage. But I knew that it was just a matter of time before it did.

Nonetheless, I was enthralled by Bill. When he kissed me for the first time, I suddenly understood what a kiss really felt like and melted. Besides, he was fun, outrageous, and would do anything to get attention. (A bit like Marty, really.)

One time, he even drove his Cadillac right into the lake. After I took him to my senior prom, that same night he actually asked me to help him clean up the bar in his father's restaurant because he had promised his father that he would.

So Red and I and Bill and Roy all ended up cleaning Bill's father's bar with scrub buckets and mops, laughing, playing the jukebox, joking and falling all over the place, still dressed in our formal prom gowns and elegant tuxedos. That same evening, I tasted my first glass of wine, and Bill and I had a great time together. Every single moment I was with Bill, we had a great time together.

That great time didn't include sex, though. Sure, we petted, but there wasn't any question of my jumping into bed with Bill. I wasn't that kind of girl. Casual sex just didn't interest me. I was determined to wait until I fell in love and got married and then lost my virginity with my husband.

None of which didn't mean that I wasn't sexy. Quite the reverse. I was born highly sexed, even though I didn't realize it at that time. I was that and more, but I would only discover the truth about my supercharged sexuality much later, with my first husband, Jack Cassidy.

But Bill and I had so much fun together. I was attracted to him physically, he was funny and sophisticated, and everything about him intrigued me. Red and I often double-dated with Bill and Roy, all in a whirl of theaters and fancy restaurants.

I fell for Bill quickly, but there was still the matter of Lou, and I felt guilty. So I sat down and wrote Lou a classic, heartfelt Dear John, telling him how much I respected him, and how I knew that he was going to become the most worthy citizen ever and win all kinds of awards, but that I thought that show business was going to be my life.

Then I took a deep breath and wrote more, confessing the rest of the truth: *I've met a young man that I'm dating now.*

I had been honest in my letter to Lou and braced myself to face the consequences of my words. Sure enough, Lou was devastated. He wrote back, *I am so sorry you feel this way,* and much, much more, all in the same vein, which made me feel extremely guilty.

Worse still, a few days after Lou received my letter, his mother stormed over to our house and said, "How dare you do this to my son! He's trying to make his way in the world and he's doing so well, and you absolutely devastated him. How could you do it?"

I felt awful. From that moment on, whenever Lou's mother saw me walking down the street (which was often, as we lived across from each other), she walked the other way. It was dreadful, but that's how it was.

Through the years, though, I watched Lou's professional progress from afar with great pride and affection. He served with honor in Vietnam, won medals, then married and later had six children, became a doctor, the assistant to the Surgeon General, and even operated on former President Eisenhower.

During the early eighties, I was booked to perform in Maryland, and Lou got wind of it and wrote to me, asking me to visit. So I called him when I arrived, and we met at a little outdoor restaurant and reminisced about old times together.

Although I'd jilted Lou all those years ago, he was still lovely to me and said how proud he was of me. In return, I told him how proud I was of him, of all the things he had achieved, and how heroic he had been in Vietnam.

Soon after, I found out that he had terminal cancer. I was utterly devastated. A while later, I was scheduled to be in Washington, so I called Lou's wife and arranged to stop by and see him.

When I arrived at his house, he came out to meet me dressed in full military uniform and invited me in. His wife left us alone together. He introduced me to two of his children, then he brought down lots of scrapbooks and showed me pictures of his family.

We didn't have long together, as I had a plane to catch, and I told Lou that I was so sorry about his condition and that I wished I could stay with him longer.

He walked me to my car but, in the middle of the driveway, stopped short and said, "Before you go, Shirley, I have something to tell you. I have never stopped loving you."

The tears flowed for both of us.

I kissed him good-bye, then left.

He passed away two weeks later.

Afterward, I sent his wife back the plebe pin along with a note telling her that I felt it belonged to her.

She sent me a long note, along with a scrapbook he had kept about me, and all the letters I had written to him through the years.

I thought you should have this scrapbook, so that you will always have it as a memory of how he felt about you, she wrote.

* * *

Back when I was dating Bill, my relationship with him had grown hotter (but it still didn't include sex). Consumed by passion and a sense of adventure, one crazy day when I was sixteen years old, I suggested to him that we drive across the border to Maryland and get married there.

My suggestion wasn't as romantic as it sounded, though. Red and Roy were with us, and my plan was that all four of us would take the plunge and get married over the border, together.

We drove across the state line and were just fifteen minutes away from arriving at the justice of the peace's office when, fortunately for my future and theirs, Bill, Red, and Roy talked me out of my madcap idea, and we turned around and drove back to Smithton.

Soon after, Bill and I broke up. My suggestion, not his. Preceded, of course, by my Dear John. I was getting quite good at these letters and felt quite in control of my loves and my life. But pride, as they say, comes before a fall. For I was yet to meet my Waterloo, my first husband, the love of my life, Jack Cassidy.

Bill Boninni and I stayed in touch through the years, and when I was performing at Heinz Hall in Pittsburgh in 1958, he turned up at the stage door after my first show. We talked about our past together, and Bill told me he was happily married, and I was glad. Three years later, he died.

* * *

In 1952, while Bill and I were still dating, my singing teacher, Ralph Lewando came up with a revolutionary idea. Or so it seemed to me at the time. He suggested that I enter the Miss Pittsburgh pageant, and sing an aria as my talent.

It wasn't that he considered me to be "cheesecake" material. His suggestion was motivated by the pageant's prize: a two-year scholarship to the drama school at the Pittsburgh Playhouse.

So I followed Ralph's advice, gritted my teeth, and entered the Miss Pittsburgh pageant, which was the preliminary contest leading to Miss America. And, despite my misgivings, my parents, who, as always, were solidly behind my career choices, encouraged me.

I never dreamed that I had any chance of winning the contest. I didn't have a model-girl figure, or high cheekbones, so I didn't think that I was a beauty-queen type at all. I was just an all-American girl, not a smoldering, sultry beauty like Marlene Dietrich. Apart from which, I was the youngest girl entering the contest that year.

I sang Arditi's beautiful aria "Il Bacio" and, to my everlasting amazement, won the contest, the two-year scholarship to the Pittsburgh Playhouse drama school, plus $500 and a gold charm bracelet. After that, I made some personal appearances and then entered the Miss

Pennsylvania competition and came in second.

Winning the Miss Pittsburgh pageant, then getting the opportunity to study at the Pittsburgh Playhouse, should have been a dream come true for me. But strangely enough, I had mixed feelings about spending two years studying singing and drama; sure, I wanted to be a Broadway star. But more than that, I still wanted to be a veterinarian.

In the summer of 1953, after my high school graduation, I was still torn between my Broadway ambitions and my dream of becoming a vet. At which point, my mother gave me the best advice she had ever offered me: go to junior college and then make up your mind which career path to follow.

So I signed up for Centenary Junior College in Hackettstown, New Jersey, figuring that my mother was right.

I was due to start college in September, and in July, my parents and I took our usual trip to Manhattan, and to Broadway.

Then, as they say, fate intervened.

The three of us were staying at the Taft Hotel, and, on a whim, I called a friend, Ken Welch, who was the former musical director of the Pittsburgh Playhouse. One thing led to another, and before I knew it, Ken and I were running through some numbers, while he accompanied us on his piano. He even took the time to compose a song especially for me, "My Very First Kiss." Then, because he believed in my talent so strongly, he went out on a limb and introduced me to Broadway agent Gus Schirmer (a member of the illustrious G. Schirmer publishing dynasty). Gus signed me up on the spot and uttered the sentence that would change my life: "Rodgers and Hammerstein's casting director is having an open audition at the St. James Theatre today. Why don't you go along?"

Well, I was very young, I had no Broadway experience, and I had never been to an audition in my life. But I was game for anything, so I plunged straight in and decided to attend the audition.

The wings of the St. James Theatre, just off Broadway, were packed that morning with nearly one hundred singers and dancers, all set on being cast in a Rodgers and Hammerstein show—any one of them. Rodgers and Hammerstein, the geniuses of the musical theater, had so many shows running simultaneously on Broadway and throughout the country at that time that they had to replace chorus people constantly.

During their legendary careers, which changed the course of American musical theater, the iconic duo Rodgers (who wrote the music) and Hammerstein (who wrote the lyrics) created a string of hit musicals from *Oklahoma!* to *The Sound of Music*, not to mention *Carousel*, *South Pacific*, and *The King and I*—and won a stupendous thirty-four Tony Awards, fifteen Academy Awards, and the Pulitzer Prize.

So here I was, Shirley Jones from Smithton, Pennsylvania, standing alone on the stage at the St. James Theatre, in front of Rodgers and Hammerstein's casting director, about to sing for all I was worth. After all, I had nothing to lose, so I went for broke and sang "The Best Things in Life Are Free." When I finished, a voice from the auditorium shouted out some abrupt questions: "Where are you from? And what have you done before?"

"Smithton," I stammered, "and nothing."

I later discovered the voice belonged to Rodgers and Hammerstein's respected casting director, John Fearnley. "Haven't you been in any shows?" he went on.

I shook my head.

"Then have you got something else prepared?"

I had.

I launched straight into my second number, Rodgers and Hart's "Lover," which I sang in a high key.

To my surprise, John Fearnley asked me to sing a third song. Luckily, I had come prepared with "My Very First Kiss," the song Kenny had written just for me.

After I'd finished, there was a moment's silence from the auditorium, during which I wished the stage would open up and swallow me right then and there.

Finally, three words rang out that would change my life: "I'm very impressed."

Then John Fearnley asked me to wait. "Mr. Rodgers happens to be across the street rehearsing the orchestra for *Oklahoma!* at City Center. I would like to have him hear you," he said.

I was so excited that he liked me that I didn't even catch the name of the man for whom I was supposed to sing next. I waited a few minutes, then there was a rustling in the stalls as a second man joined Fearnley in the auditorium.

At Fearnley's request, I sang the same three songs over again, and then a voice rang out: "You have a beautiful voice, young lady."

"Thank you, Mr. . . . Mr. . . ."

"Mr. Richard Rodgers, my dear."

Whenever I tell the story of what happened next at the master classes I sometimes give for young people at universities, I cringe with embarrassment at how quickly and easily everything unfolded for me. It was as if a magician had waved his wand and effortlessly raised the curtain on my career.

"Could you wait twenty minutes?" Richard Rodgers asked me. "I'm going to call my partner, Oscar Hammerstein, who is at home. I would like to have Mr. Hammerstein hear you sing."

I shot a glance at Kenny, who shook his head and dropped a bombshell on me: He couldn't accompany me because he had to leave for the airport in a couple of minutes to catch a plane. I explained this to Mr. Rodgers.

"No problem," Richard Rodgers said. "You can sing with the symphony orchestra."

I had never seen a symphony orchestra, never mind sung with one. But, as I said, I was game for anything. Ten minutes later, I was standing in front of a real-life symphony orchestra, about to sing to the most famous Broadway-musical-theater team of all time.

In retrospect, my saving grace that day was that I thought this kind of thing happened ten times a day on Broadway. I assumed lots of unknown kids with no experience walked in off the street and ended up singing for Rodgers and Hammerstein. Had I known that I had got a break in a billion, I would have been overcome by an avalanche of nerves, but as I didn't, I was not.

"Miss Jones, do you know the score to *Oklahoma!*?" Mr. Hammerstein asked.

"I know the music, but I don't know all the words," I said, probably committing the gaffe of a lifetime, as Hammerstein was the lyricist. Fortunately, I was oblivious.

I was handed the score, and, as the gravity of the moment started to dawn on me, I held it right in front of my face, so that I wouldn't have to look at either Rodgers or Hammerstein. Then I launched into "People Will Say We're in Love," followed by "Oh, What a Beautiful Morning."

Mr. Rodgers thanked me and went into a corner, where he conferred with Mr. Hammerstein in a hushed voice.

"Miss Jones, what are your plans?" Mr. Rodgers called out from the auditorium after a short while.

"I'm starting college in a couple of weeks, Mr. Rodgers."

"Miss Jones, we would like to make you an offer," Mr. Rodgers said. "We have a spot for you in the chorus of *South Pacific*."

I accepted his offer without a moment's hesitation and, soon after, with Gus Schirmer's help and advice, became the only performer ever to be put under contract to Rodgers and Hammerstein. A seven-year contract, no less! My future as a Broadway musical star, it seemed, was assured.

So that's how it all began.

I owed it all to Richard Rodgers. He was my fairy godfather, and I was grateful.

Well, perhaps not as grateful as he hoped I would be.

A year after my first audition with Richard Rodgers and Oscar Hammerstein, I was cast in the movie version of *Oklahoma!* and was being hailed as "Hollywood's new Cinderella." Mr. Rodgers invited me into his office and made a cold-blooded pass at me.

I was shocked, but I somehow had the presence of mind to say, "You are very kind, Mr. Rodgers"—removing his pudgy hand from my knee—"and I will always think of you as my grandfather."

It is a tribute to Richard Rodgers's professionalism that he didn't take steps to fire me or ensure *Oklahoma!* was the last movie I would ever make.

With my parents' support and encouragement, I moved into the Barbizon Hotel for Women, on the corner of Lexington and East Sixty-Third, where Grace Kelly, Joan Crawford, and Gene Tierney had stayed at the start of their careers, and I lived there for a year.

Meanwhile, on Rodgers and Hammerstein's instructions, I observed *South Pacific* for three weeks before joining the show, which at that time was in the last six months of its Broadway run. I was paid the massive sum of $120 a week and cast as a nurse in the chorus. I did some dancing and had just one line in the show: "What's the trouble, Knucklehead?"

I danced in the "I'm in Love with a Wonderful Guy" scene as well as in "There Is Nothing Like a Dame." The chorus guys were terrific and I loved every minute of my time in the show.

After that, Rodgers and Hammerstein cast me in the last six weeks of the Chicago run of *Me and Juliet*, a play within a play, revolving around a backstage romance. *Me and Juliet* was set in a Broadway theater where *Me and Juliet* was being produced. It's been likened to the concept behind

A Chorus Line, but *Me and Juliet* was before its time. It turned out to be one of Rodgers and Hammerstein's rare failures.

Although my roles in these shows were minor, Rodgers and Hammerstein didn't forget me. They arranged for me to study in the daytime with an acting coach and a vocal coach, and at night I was understudy to leading lady Isabel Bigley, who sang the great American standard "No Other Love." I also danced in the chorus, and with me was another Shirley, a Shirley who was my polar opposite in every single way.

Five foot seven, with a pixie haircut and a surprisingly strong voice, Shirley MacLaine first turned her attention on me on the day when she discovered that I was scheduled to fly to Hollywood to screen-test for the part of Laurey in the movie version of *Oklahoma!*

"Get me the part of Ado Annie. I am Ado Annie," she demanded, and gave me a hearty pat on the back.

"But, Shirley, I don't have the job yet. I can't tell Rodgers and Hammerstein who to hire," I said in what I thought was a reasonable voice.

"But I have to play Ado Annie. I am Ado Annie," Shirley shrieked, unafraid to ally herself with the flirt from *Oklahoma!* who just "cain't say no."

"I'll definitely mention your name."

Later, I lived up to my promise and did suggest

that Shirley MacLaine be considered for the part of Ado Annie, but she did not get the part. Gloria Grahame did, but Shirley, of course, sailed on to other, better things.

Many years later, Marty and I were in a charity performance of *It's a Wonderful Life* at the Geffen Playhouse, along with Annette Bening, who is married to Shirley's brother, Warren Beatty.

After the show, Shirley and Warren were outside waiting for Annette, when Shirley saw me.

"There she is, Shirley Jones! We were in our first show together," Shirley screamed to all and sundry.

In contrast, Warren said nothing and shot me a smile.

Years before he married Annette, I was coming out of Saks Fifth Avenue, in Beverly Hills, when Warren, always a world-class Casanova, strolled up to me and said, "You are so beautiful. Would you go out with me?"

"I'm married, Warren," I said, surprised that he didn't know.

"That doesn't make any difference." He sounded genuinely surprised that I would for even one second consider my marital status the slightest impediment to our embarking on a liaison.

As poised and exuberant as Shirley MacLaine was and is, in recent years I managed to surprise her soon after I'd stopped dying my hair and let it go naturally white.

Shirley took one look at me, and her eyes widened in shock and she said, "Shirley Jones, that's *very* brave of you. I take my hat off to you. You've got a lot of guts to let your hair go white in this business."

My stint in *Me and Juliet* was memorable for me because Sari Price was in the cast and would become my lifelong friend.

One other bright and shining memory from the run of the show: one morning, out of the blue, I received a telephone call from my mother informing me that my father was on the way to see *Me and Juliet* and spend time with me in Chicago.

"But Daddy is scared of flying!" I said. (Come to think of it, so is Marty. Strange how the people we love often exhibit similar traits and phobias. . . .)

My father was, indeed, petrified of flying. But the depth of his love for me was such that he braved the flight from Pittsburgh to Chicago and showed up at the hotel where Sari and I were staying.

Sari was instantly captivated by him, particularly when he asked us what we wanted to do the next day. We told him we'd both been longing to experience Chicago's beautiful parks, and he immediately hired a car to take us there and then to lunch afterward.

In the evening, after the show, he came with us to the next-door piano bar and bought beer for us and all the kids who worked with us. It was so cute.

I was sad when he left but promised to come home for a visit as soon as I could. Soon after he left, I received a memorable telephone call from my agent, Gus Schirmer. "Hello, Laurey!" he said. Against all odds, I had won the part of Laurey Williams in the movie version of *Oklahoma!*

I was ecstatic. Soon after, I went home to Smithton to see my parents, and I met the first movie star I'd ever encountered in my life—the inimitable, the notorious, the once-in-a-lifetime legend Mae West.

I'd always been fascinated by Mae. I had been named Shirley Mae Jones, but the Mae was after one of my mother's sisters, not Miss West. But that didn't stop everyone who—even today—ever heard my middle name from assuming that I was named after Mae West.

When I learned that Mae West was appearing in person at a nightclub called Twin Coaches, which was on a little country road in Belle Vernon, a mile from Smithton, I immediately booked to see the show. Belle Vernon being a small town like Smithton, someone must have seen me buying the tickets for Mae's show, as soon after, I received a telephone call from one of her assistants inviting me backstage to see her after the show.

It was summer, and that day the temperature had climbed to a sweltering one hundred degrees and rising. When I was taken backstage to see Mae, I discovered her lying on a couch, half-naked, with a fur coat draped over her. Tentatively, I asked if she would pose for a photograph with me.

Mae looked me up and down. "Honey, where's your fur?"

"I don't have my fur with me, Miss West. It's summer."

Mae pulled herself up to her full height (which wasn't much, despite her towering high heels). "I don't take photos without a fur, and nor should you." She stalked over to the closet, pulled out a fur coat, and flung it at me. "Put that on, then we'll take a photo together."

I did. And was photographed with Mae West.

Just me and Mae, side by side. In furs!

My audience with Mae West, however, was not an accident. When she learned that I was coming to see her show, she specifically asked to meet me and invited me backstage afterward.

Mae West was a legend, a movie star, and world famous.

And me? I was Shirley Mae Jones, a chorus girl from a small town in Pennsylvania, who'd never made a movie in her life.

But that was the moment when all that was about to change. Mae invited me backstage to see her in her dressing room because she knew it.

The news of my casting as Laurey in *Oklahoma!* had spread like wildfire, promoted by the Rodgers and Hammerstein organization itself, in the world press: it was the story of a small-town Cinderella bound for Hollywood and stardom. Mae West had read about me, and hence my invitation.

As far as the world had been told, I was now that fairy-tale heroine, and I was destined to live happily ever after on the silver screen—and off.

All that remained was for this Cinderella to meet her Prince Charming.

THREE

A Wonderful Feeling

Winning the part of Laurey in *Oklahoma!* was every young actress's dream, but for me, the making of the movie turned out to be a nightmare.

Based on the play *Green Grow the Lilacs* by Lynn Riggs, *Oklahoma!* is the story of settlers in Oklahoma's Indian territories and centers around farm girl Laurey Williams and her two suitors, the good-natured cowboy Curly McLain and the saturnine farmhand Jud Fry.

Oklahoma! had been Rodgers and Hammerstein's biggest Broadway hit so far and was now going to be their first movie together. Consequently, both of them were determined that the movie version of *Oklahoma!* would equal, or even surpass, the show's success.

To that end, they oversaw every detail of the $6.8 million movie from start to finish. *Oklahoma!* may have been the world's first Todd-AO 70 mm production, masterminded by Mike Todd, who had invented the new wide-screen process, but Rodgers and Hammerstein were set on stamping their mark on every single scene, every single performance, in the movie. Which meant that the intensity of their focus on me—as the movie's leading lady and Hollywood's latest Cinderella—was obsessive in the extreme.

I knew they had given me a once-in-a-lifetime opportunity and that I was more than lucky to be playing Laurey. Moreover, they were paying me the princely sum of $500 a week, a fortune in today's money.

So I made up my mind not to be difficult and to go along with whatever they required of me. So although I was furious when they decreed that my upper lip be waxed because it had a smidgen of peach fuzz on it, I gritted my teeth and submitted to it.

I might not have been so malleable had I known that the procedure was going to be so painful (and, at the time, primitive). First the beautician smeared the hot wax on my upper lip, then ripped off the wax and the hair with it, after which she left ice cubes on my upper lip for thirty minutes. I was in agony, and furious when the fuzz grew back darker than before, which meant that I had to have electrolysis, which I hated.

When the next decree came down from on high that I should have all my teeth capped because of a gap between two of them, I flatly refused, and Rodgers and Hammerstein backed off and changed the lighting instead. Not a great start to my first movie, which everyone, including me, had believed would be straight out of a fairy tale for me.

I was thrilled, though, when I learned that director Fred Zinnemann, of *High Noon* and *From Here to Eternity* fame, would be directing me in this, my first movie. Luckily for me, Zinnemann would live up to his reputation as a talented director with a brilliant instinct for bringing out the best in his actresses.

After our first scene together, he asked me if I had ever acted in front of a camera before.

Stricken, and afraid that my inexperience had shown, I shook my head, crestfallen.

"Don't change anything. You're a natural," the great Fred Zinnemann said, to my relief.

I had assumed that the movie would be shot in Oklahoma, but then Zinnemann realized that present-day Oklahoma had far too many oil wells dotted about the landscape to pass for 1906, the year in which the story was set.

Instead, he settled on Nogales in Arizona's San Rafael Valley and set about re-creating Oklahoma there. Three months before shooting began, a crew was sent ahead to plant ten acres of wheat and corn, to move sod and peach trees, so that the terrain would resemble that of Oklahoma. Then the crew built a barn, a silo, a windmill, and a farmhouse.

In July 1954, the three-hundred-strong cast and

crew of *Oklahoma!* moved to Nogales and shooting began. Little did I know that for the next nine months, I'd be working a fifteen-hour day, seven days a week. Actors, you see, didn't have a union in those days battling for them to work equitable hours.

Consequently, my day during filming routinely began at four thirty in the morning and ended late at night. I didn't mind the hard work, though I did now and again ask myself if I wanted to work that hard for the rest of my life. But I loved the script and adored the songs, and working with Gordon MacRae was heaven. I adored him at first sight and even developed a mild crush on him as filming went on, but took great pains to fight it.

Rod Steiger, however, was another story. A Method actor, the acclaimed star of *On the Waterfront* and a perfect foil to Marlon Brando, Rod, a handsome if eccentric character, was also somewhat of a ladies' man. Though married to an actress named Sally Gracie, that didn't prevent him from making a play for other women whenever he felt like it.

He was nine years older than me, and while he didn't exactly make a physical pass at me as Richard Rodgers had, he asked a great many leading questions that left me with no doubt whatsoever about his true intentions toward me.

"Are you one of those girls who wants to wait

until you are married before you do anything?" was his opening gambit.

"Perhaps," I said.

More questions followed. "Have you ever had an affair with a man?" Rod asked.

I knew what he meant. Had I ever been to bed with a man? Had I ever had sexual intercourse? I hadn't, and I told him so.

Undeterred (or perhaps spurred on) by my innocence, Rod said, "Well, then, would you like to have your first affair with me?"

I shook my head.

"Why not? What's the matter with you?"

I didn't answer.

That was Rod Steiger's one and only attempt at seducing me. Afterward, I discovered that the canny Fred Zinnemann had taken Rod aside and asked him to take care of me because I was so young. Chastened, Rod agreed. Fortunately for me, he was enough of a gentleman never to break his word to Zinnemann.

Soon after, he approached me somewhat sheepishly and said with a question implicit in his voice, "I was told that you are very young and that I mustn't do anything to upset you. . . ."

"You didn't," I said, and the subject was closed. Rod and I ended getting along so well that after filming finished and he was cast to play Jud in the European stage tour in which I would be playing Laurey again, I was delighted. So, too, initially, was the tour's director, Rouben Mamoulian, who had directed the Broadway version of *Oklahoma!* and, as a movie director, was much beloved by Marlene Dietrich, Greta Garbo, and Hedy Lamarr.

However, experienced as Mamoulian, a fiery Armenian, was as a director, during rehearsals he was in for a surprise when he encountered Rod Steiger's unusual acting technique. Unprepared for Rod's Lee Strasberg style of Method acting and Rod's tendency to mumble (more pronounced onstage than in the movie), he kept yelling for Rod to speak up. Rod studiously ignored him.

Worse still, in the smokehouse scene when Rod, as Jud, clashes with Gordon MacRae, as Curly, Rod suddenly pulled out an apple and chomped loudly on it right through the whole scene.

Enraged, Mamoulian yelled, "Get out of my theater! Get out of my life!"

Stunned, Rod said, "What the hell is the matter with you?"

"You're fired!"

Poor Rod never did understand why.

I guess I should have taken note of the negative aspect of Rod's much-vaunted Method training but probably didn't, as years later I considered training at Lee Strasberg's Actors Studio, the bastion of the Method system, myself.

Fortunately, before I was due to make a final commitment to the Actors Studio, I was invited to sit and watch eight classes there. As I studied

Lee Strasberg and his approach to his hapless students, I was appalled. One student was instructed by Strasberg to pretend to be a dog and lick the floor beneath his paws. He complied.

Another student was told to imagine that he had blood running down his chest, while Lee Strasberg conducted a nonstop monologue. Nothing Strasberg said had any connection with the play the actor was appearing in, or the character he was playing.

I quickly concluded that the Actors Studio approach was not for me. I much preferred the Bette Davis school of acting. She was kept waiting one day to do her scene at the Studio while another actor interminably discussed his motivations for taking off his shoe, his mood, his emotions.

In the end, an exasperated Bette burst out, "Just drop it on the floor. It's only a goddamn shoe!"

I agreed with Bette. After observing my fourth class at the Actors Studio, I walked out. The Actors Studio and Method acting were definitely not me.

Although I didn't know it at the time, at the start of the filming of *Oklahoma!* Oscar Hammerstein was worried that I might put on weight and enlisted Charlotte Greenwood, then in her sixties, who played Aunt Eller in the movie, to monitor my eating.

With her encouragement, I began to eat a little less. But after I was caught committing the cardinal sin of tucking into a cherry pie during lunch break, Fred Zinnemann (probably at Oscar Hammerstein's behest) suggested that it was time for me to quit eating desserts and go on a diet instead.

Now, I had been raised on home-cooked meals and didn't have a clue about counting calories and embarking on diets, but I quickly got the picture. I didn't like the look of it, but I agreed and cut down on the desserts for a start.

That still wasn't enough for Oscar. A few days later, he sat me down and said, "Shirley, you've put on a pound or two, my dear. It looks as if Gloria Grahame is sending you care packages."

The intimation was clear: although Gloria, a glamorous MGM star who had appeared as the temptress Violet in *It's a Wonderful Life*, was cast as Ado Annie, and not Laurey, if I didn't toe the line, our roles could swiftly be switched, and I would be relegated to playing Annie, and Gloria given my part of Laurey, instead.

So I braced myself and started my diet. Only back then, there wasn't much publicity about diets, and while I was supposed to go on one—a crash diet at that—I didn't get any guidance or any vitamins to help me through it. So I just used my own judgment. From then on, I lived on grapefruit and toast and nothing else. Literally.

I dropped ten pounds so fast that it made my head spin. A week later, on the MGM backlot in Hollywood, where we were filming the country bath scene, which was shot in an ice-cold pond, I passed out from hunger.

Problem was, no one knew the reason. And Hollywood being Hollywood, and gossip being gossip, word spread like wildfire that I was pregnant. Luckily for me, my hairdresser became party to all the cruel gossip and sprang to my defense: "This little girl is as pure as the snow on a Christmas roof. The poor thing hasn't eaten in a week, and no wonder she has fainted!"

Everyone got the message, and so did I. The next day was my day off, so I sneaked out, bought about ten candy bars, and ate every single one of them!

When it came down to it, I felt more comfortable with the *Oklahoma!* crew than with the cast. To me, my fellow actors were too self-involved, and the crew was more real, more like the people I grew up with in Smithton. Small-town people with values and integrity.

The crew must have reciprocated my affection because, at the end of the picture, they presented me with a gold chain with a beautiful gold disk hanging from it that was engraved with SHIRLEY JONES, BLESS YOUR BONES. YOUR CREW. That was the best moment of the entire shoot for me.

As soon as filming of *Oklahoma!* finished, in a strange publicity maneuver, Rodgers and Hammerstein decided to dispatch me all over the country to promote the movie—even though it wasn't due to be released for a whole year. So without much briefing or advice on how to handle the press, I set off on the promotion tour for *Oklahoma!*—during which I was subjected to interviews with publications like the *New Yorker*, *Newsweek*, often in opulent settings.

One reporter wined and dined me at Sardi's, but rather ruined my enjoyment of my surroundings by greeting me: "Shirley Jones! At least you could have changed your name. I mean, what could be so simple, Shirley Jones from Smithton, Pennsylvania."

Richard Rodgers had said the same thing to me, way back when we first met, and I'd resisted his blandishments that I change my name. So this time around, I was prepared with an answer: "Well, I wanted to change it to Shirley Smith from Jonestown, but they wouldn't let me."

The reporter was not impressed and afterward complained to *Oklahoma!*'s publicity guy, Nick Pachukis, "She may be the Cinderella Girl, but she's as dull as dishwater."

Until then, I'd led an extremely sheltered life. What exactly did everyone expect from me? But I refused to be downhearted and soldiered on, spreading the word about the movie, full of enthusiasm for it, all genuine and heartfelt, and did the job to the best of my ability.

Oklahoma! opened at the Rivoli Theatre in Manhattan on October 13, 1955. Tickets cost a stratospheric $3.50 ($45 in today's terms), and the movie played there for a whole year.

Overflowing with excitement, I attended the Los Angeles premiere with my parents, all of us riding to the theater together in a surrey with a fringe on the top.

When the lights went down, and I saw the words *Introducing Shirley Jones* and then my face, bigger than life, up on the screen, I was over-whelmed. I was young, naïve, and, until then, still hadn't quite grasped the enormity of what had happened to me. One audition and here I was, starring in one of the biggest movies ever made.

The next morning, my reviews were uniformly wonderful, with one glaring exception. Given that Hollywood columnist Louella Parsons was firmly in my camp, it meant that Louella's rival Hedda Hopper would automatically be whole-heartedly against me.

Hedda Hopper snarled in her review of me, "She's a one-time Charlie. She's pretty and she sings well, but it's a one-picture deal for this girl. She's never going to work again."

In contrast, my review from Louella was glowing and included, "This girl is going to be the biggest star in Hollywood." The lines between America's top Hollywood columnists were drawn. From then on, Louella would always be in my camp, on my side, and Hedda, against me. At the time, I remember thinking that even if they both agreed about me, or if they reversed their positions, I would survive. Louella or Hedda? It was rather like deciding which one of your veins you wanted your doctor to open.

As soon as *Oklahoma!* had its premiere, Rodgers and Hammerstein sent me out on yet another national tour to promote it. During the tour, journalist after journalist interviewed me about every aspect of my life, and I answered every question truthfully. Except one. Did I have a man in my life?

I always shook my head no, when, of course, I did.

Flashback to May 1955. Six weeks of rehearsals for the European tour of *Oklahoma!* were due to begin in a New York theater, but before they started, I was issued with a dire warning about Jack Cassidy, the man who would be playing Curly to my Laurey in the show.

"I know he's handsome, I know he's talented. I know he's playing your leading man. But don't, whatever you do, fall in love with him, Shirley," said Selma Linch, my agent, Gus Schirmer's right-hand woman. "Every girl does. Just remember that he's married."

She meant so well, Selma did. She just didn't know that I was—and would always be—the kind of girl who did exactly the opposite of what she was asked, a headstrong girl who flew in the face of advice and went against convention, with her eyes fixed firmly on the next adventure.

And what an adventure!

Jack Cassidy, my costar in the European tour of *Oklahoma!*, was a dashing Broadway star, startlingly handsome with white-blond hair and hypnotic blue Irish eyes, a world-class charmer, who glittered with sexuality, sparkled with charisma, and exuded a sense of danger, overlaid with a suave sophistication far beyond his years, and certainly mine.

The quintessential matinee idol, Jack was urbane, elegant, debonair, and oozed style from every pore. A big spender: money meant nothing to him. As he once characterized it to his son, David, "Money is only green paper." Buttressed by his cavalier attitude toward finances, Jack wore $1,000 suits during a time when that sum of money could buy a Volkswagen.

He was a dandy, a clotheshorse, and his image always meant far more to him than anything— or anyone—else in his life. According to David Cassidy, his mother, Evelyn, was heard to complain that if Jack had $50 in his pocket, he would give her $10 with which to feed herself and David and spend the other $40 on a suit for himself. Throughout, Jack's extravagance knew no bounds, and later on in his life his limo bill routinely ran $3,000 a week and he was also the proud owner of 104 pairs of handmade shoes.

To top all that, Jack was extremely knowledgeable about art, literature, interior decorating, gourmet food, fashion, and—above all, as I was to discover—sex.

Not bad for the son of a railroad engineer from Jamaica, Queens, New York, who was one of five children (the youngest of which died in childhood) and came from a tough, working-class Irish-German background.

Jack's father, Willy Cassidy, was a charming but feckless man, a womanizer and a drunk. In contrast, his mother, Lotte (short for Charlotte), from Hamburg, Germany, was said to have veins filled with ice and to be tough as nails. She was forty-eight when she gave birth to Jack and never forgave him for being a change-of-life child. She neither wanted nor loved him. Jack told me that his mother had farmed him out to a next-door neighbor and had never shown him any kindness or affection.

Lotte beat him relentlessly and made him work around the house for hours, cleaning every surface until it shone to perfection. Finally, instead of rebelling against his mother's house-proud ways, Jack grew up to become as much of a clean freak as she was, which later caused problems when he was living in a household with three raucous, normal, untidy sons.

Jack may have capitulated in the face of his mother's insistence on cleanliness above everything else, but he never forgave her for her cruel treatment of him. When she was on her deathbed and begged him to return to the Church (which he had long since rejected), he refused. Nor did he go to her funeral. All of that led to great guilt, and down the line, the guilt that Jack felt about his mother would ultimately rise up and destroy him.

As a small boy, Jack also had a hard time at school. As he wasn't as big as the other kids, he was forced to either fight them or slip them a few dimes to stop them from beating him up. Life was tough for him. So, like many kids who want to take refuge from the rough-and-tumble of their backgrounds, he escaped into the movies. When he saw handsome, legendary matinee idol John Barrymore up there on the silver screen, Jack knew what he wanted to be when he grew up. He wanted to be John Barrymore, plain and simple.

Ambitious and determined to succeed in the big, wide world, Jack, by the time he was eleven years old, was already delivering ice and coal around the neighborhood and at various times worked as a bellhop, a dishwasher, a clerk, and a stable-boy. Then, when he was only sixteen years old, he made his Broadway debut in the chorus of Cole Porter's *Something for the Boys* and began his theatrical career in earnest.

Appearing in a Cole Porter show was the height of Broadway success for a performer. Born in 1891, Cole wrote some of the most iconic songs in the Great American songbook. "Let's Do It (Let's Fall in Love)," "Begin the Beguine," "You Do Something to Me," "Night and Day," and "I Get a Kick out of You" were only some of them. To quote Cole Porter himself, in terms of Broadway stardom, he was "the tops."

Exactly how Jack made it into Cole Porter's *Something for the Boys* at the age of sixteen is another story, the details of which I learned later on in my relationship with Jack. By that time, I was already so beguiled by Jack that nothing about him, not even the real story of how he made it to Broadway at such an early age, would ever shock me.

That first day at rehearsals in Manhattan, in response to Selma's warnings regarding Jack, coupled with further scuttlebutt about him fed to me by the rest of the cast, I steeled myself to be impervious to his much-vaunted charm, to be oblivious of his good looks, his sex appeal, his charisma. A piece of cake, I told myself, particu-

74

larly as Jack Cassidy was bound to be full of himself like most actors and wouldn't be worth knowing at all.

Besides, I'd caught a glimpse of him making a call in the backstage phone booth and decided he was way too pretty and definitely not my type of man. That, coupled with the warnings I'd been given about him, made me predisposed to dislike him.

But when he strode across the stage toward me, held out his hand diffidently, and said, "Hi, I'm Jack Cassidy. It's a pleasure to be working with you," I was utterly unprepared for just how nice Jack was. Nor was I prepared for his talent, either, when we sang our first song together, "People Will Say We're in Love."

The chemistry between us was so palpable, even during that very first duet together, that our jaded European director, Rouben Mamoulian, virtually cracked his whip and snapped, "Now, now, darlings, we only fall in love in the play. It is only onstage that we do this. Do not take this with you outside."

Jack and I joined the rest of the cast in laughing, but both of us were laughing a trifle uneasily. I had already floated up onto cloud nine and was firmly under Jack's spell, not just the seductive spell of Jack the man, but the potent spell of Jack Cassidy the singer and the performer.

Rather than gush all over the page about just

how great a singer and a performer Jack was, I'll quote distinguished *New York Times* critic Clive Barnes and his seasoned judgment of Jack's 1975 performance in the play *Murder Among Friends*: "Stormily brilliant . . . he walks on the set wearing his ego like a cloak and his mind like a dagger."

I was overwhelmed by the beauty of Jack's voice that day and felt for a moment that my own voice was wanting. I confided in Jack that I didn't think I hit certain notes properly, and he said, "You have a beautiful voice, but you close up on certain notes. You need to open up more." In the most tactful way possible, Jack had given me a singing lesson, and it was a revelation to me.

From the first, the nicest part about Jack was that, unlike other men, he didn't come on to me strong. He didn't pounce on me. He was the perfect gentleman, courtly, intelligent, and unfailingly polite.

After that first day's rehearsal, we each went our separate ways—me to my small apartment at 49 West Seventy-Third Street, which, after having moved out of the Barbizon Hotel for Young Women, I was now sharing with an actress for the vast sum of $75 a month; and Jack home to his house in West Orange, New Jersey, where he lived with his wife, dancer Evelyn Ward, and their son, David.

Evelyn, who was born in 1923 and married Jack

in 1948, was, I knew, a great beauty, a cross between Hedy Lamarr and Linda Darnell, with a similar brand of dark, exotic good looks. She was a dancer/actress who later succeeded Gwen Verdon in *New Girl in Town*, but rumor had it that she and Jack weren't happy together and that he had left her many times. "He is the ladies' man of the century" was the phrase everyone in the know always applied to Jack. I heard their words, but somehow I was undeterred and my admiration for Jack didn't diminish.

Jack and I rehearsed *Oklahoma!* together in Manhattan for six weeks before leaving for Europe and the tour, night after night gazing into each other's eyes as we sang "People Will Say We're in Love," as the sexual chemistry between us sparked, then intensified.

Three nights before the cast and crew of *Oklahoma!* were to fly to France, a party was thrown for us on an excursion ship sailing up the Hudson River. At the last minute, I decided not to take a date with me, knowing that if I had one, Jack wouldn't be able to dance with me. More than anything else in the world, I wanted to dance with Jack Cassidy that night.

My plan worked, and Jack and I danced cheek to cheek to "People Will Say We're in Love," which by now we considered to be "our song." He held me close, and the chemistry between us was palpable. I knew exactly what the cast and crew watching us were thinking, but I didn't care.

I did care, somewhat, though, for the opinion of my best friend, Sari Price, whom I'd known since *South Pacific* and who was to room with me during the European tour.

As we packed for the tour, Sari had been relentless in her warnings about Jack, a relentless prophet of doom, determined to puncture all my illusions about him: "Oh, Shirley, I'm so worried about you. He's going to break your heart. You're going to be in for a terrible time. Please, please don't fall in love with him."

I know Sari meant well and wanted only the best for me, but nothing, not even her words of wisdom, could rain on my romantic parade. I was twenty-one years old, Hollywood's Cinderella, the star of *Oklahoma!* the movie, and about to embark on the biggest adventure of my life so far—Paris in June, with the first man I'd ever met who'd truly swept me off my feet—and nothing was going to tarnish my excitement and my passion. The Paris stage of our tour—which was scheduled to go on to Rome, then London—was part of "An American Salute to France," which had been arranged by the chairman of ANTA (the American National Theatre and Academy), with the aim of enhancing the relationship between America and France. General Eisenhower himself was a major supporter of our tour and, before we left, issued a message of encouragement to all of us.

Three days later, we probably needed it. The ANTA tour was not a conventional theatrical enterprise, and everything about it turned out to be Spartan, to say the least. Which meant that instead of flying by commercial airline, we were slated to take a military transport to Paris.

The flight lasted more than twenty hours, and we all sat on the hard cabin floor, as the plane didn't have any seats in it. But we didn't care. We were flying to Paris, France, and that's all that mattered to us. So we endured the cabin floor, snacked happily on our packed lunches, and laughed a lot.

Once we were booked into our rooms in the Hotel Splendide, on the Left Bank, Sari and I were in for a shock. Our minuscule room had no closet big enough for all our clothes.

Learning of our plight, Jack offered to trade rooms with us, and we accepted, charmed by his kindness and courtesy. When Jack invited us to dinner that night, along with his roommate, a character actor of some note, Willy Kuluva, Sari and I accepted.

The European tour of *Oklahoma!* premiered at the Théâtre Champs-Élysées on June 19, 1955, with president of France, René Coty, and the US ambassador to France, Douglas Dillon, attending. Afterward, Arthur O. Sulzberger noted in the

New York Times that Jack was "a good-looking young man with a fine, rich voice," and that I "was warmly received for her portrayal."

So I was, but as the warmth of the audience cascaded over me, I was secretly nursing a special, private warmth all my own.

The warmth and romance of my first evening in Paris, with Jack Cassidy.

FOUR

Everything's Going My Way

June 18, 1955, the Tour d'Argent Restaurant, the Eiffel Tower, Paris.

I wore a white lace dress, white high heels, and my hair was pulled back in a ponytail and tied with a white ribbon. As I gazed across the table into Jack's blue eyes and then, for a second, glanced back out the window at the shimmering lights of Paris below us, I felt as if I were starring in the most romantic movie ever made.

For some unknown reason (one probably secretly engineered by Jack), Sari and Willy hadn't joined us for dinner as promised. So here I was with the notorious Jack Cassidy, sipping my first glass of champagne and supping on my first escargots.

The setting was spectacular, the atmosphere sublime, but Jack's conversation eclipsed even the high glamour of the night. Great seducer that he was, he alternated between regaling me with his own stories (working with Mary Martin, with Ethel Merman, and with Cole Porter) and asking me a myriad of questions about my life and my career.

What was it like making *Oklahoma!*? What were Rodgers and Hammerstein like? What did I think of Rod Steiger? Then on to my childhood, my family, my hopes, and my dreams.

Along the way, I told him about the Jones brewery, about Stoney's beer, and about Stoney Jones. Jack loved my stories, and from then on his secret nickname for me would be Stoney Jones, which later on he inexplicably alternated with Mouse, a strange choice of nickname, but one that I never questioned.

Jack didn't just romance me that night, he also dazzled me with his intellectual acumen. He quoted Thoreau; discussed politics, religion, and economics; and was always articulate and informative. I was enchanted, captivated, enthralled.

That night in Paris, Jack and I talked the evening away at the Tour d'Argent, then moved on to a notorious nightclub reportedly owned by one of Marlene Dietrich's lesbian lovers. There, we met Sari and Willy and danced till dawn, oblivious of how *Oklahoma!* was premiering that night and we all were expected to give the performances of our lives in the show.

At five in the morning, after dancing the night away, we all piled into a cab and headed toward our hotel. But just as the cab was about to cross the bridge over the Seine from the Right Bank to the Left Bank, Jack asked the driver to stop.

Then he turned to me and asked if I would like to get out and walk over the bridge with him. I didn't hesitate. I took his hand in mine, and in silence we walked across the bridge over the Seine, from the Right Bank to the Left, toward our hotel.

As we did, the sounds and sights of Paris assailed my senses: milkmen delivering their wares, young people on bicycles bound for home after a late night on the town, other lovers strolling along the banks of the Seine, hand in hand, as dawn broke.

It seemed to me that our walk across the Seine lasted for hours, and I never wanted it to end. I felt so close to Jack, so very close. Looking back, I believe that dawn walk with Jack, most of it done in silence, changed my life.

But overwhelmed and enchanted as I was with Jack, I still didn't consider going to bed with him that night. Instead, when we got back to our hotel, I let him walk me to the door of my room, where he gave me a chaste, light butterfly kiss. Then he looked deep into my eyes and said, "I'm going to marry you."

"But you're already married!"

"I know."

Jack then strolled down the corridor to his room.

I told myself sternly that I shouldn't for one

moment believe that Jack meant what he had said. I was fully aware that he had given me a line. I knew that I should probably at the least have been amused by him or, at worst, angry with him. Instead, somewhere deep down, I believed that Jack Cassidy meant every word he'd said to me that night and that he did intend to marry me. Or so I fervently hoped.

The next few days in Paris with Jack sped by like a heightened dream, especially when he presented me with a gold ornament of the Eiffel Tower for my charm bracelet, which he gave me as a memento of our romantic evening together.

However, when we checked out of our hotel at the end of our Paris run, I was brought down to earth from my romantic haze with somewhat of a disconcerting bump.

While I was paying my bill, Jack came up behind me and, in full earshot of some of the cast and crew said, "I hate to do this to you, Shirley, but I seem to have run out of money. Can you pay my bill?"

We had been on just one date together, but I didn't hesitate. Even though $350 was a lot of money in those days, I paid Jack's bill then and there without a second thought, while the cast and crew looked on openmouthed.

Afterward, Sari said to me, "You must be crazy! He's using you."

Perhaps. But I didn't care. Although Jack never

made the slightest attempt to pay me back, I never asked him to. He was my knight in shining armor, my prince on a white horse. I was in love with him, and I always would be.

We moved on to Rome, where, in between last-minute rehearsals, we went sightseeing like average tourists, admiring the city's memorable monuments, then spent happy hours picnicking on the beach and swimming in the Mediterranean together.

On July 9, *Oklahoma!* opened in front of a distinguished audience including the deputy prime minister of Italy, Giuseppe Saragat, Foreign Minister Gaetano Martino, and members of the Roman nobility, all of whom were so enthusiastic that they gave us eight curtain calls.

That night, after the curtain finally fell on the show, in a romantic, little Roman hotel, Jack Cassidy made love to me for the first time.

I was a virgin, having never gone "all the way" with anyone before. I had resolved to lose my virginity with the right man. That night, in Rome, I knew Jack was the right man.

He was a great lover, that night and every night afterward. He could go on for hours, have two or three orgasms, then wake up in the morning and make love to me all over again. He was inventive and extremely well endowed (a blessing that all his sons, in particular David, inherited). He had no inhibitions about sex, no barriers, and he taught me to be the same, to be free about sex and to openly want it and love it.

Through the years, Jack and I had sex wherever and whenever we wanted—on the floor of a sailboat in the middle of the Caribbean, in the dressing room at whichever theater we were appearing in, in the bathtub, and, at the height of *The Partridge Family*, now and again Jack would pick me up from the studio in the car, then drive us into the garage adjacent to our house, where he would have intercourse with me in the backseat. With me, Mrs. Partridge!

That night in Rome, the only thing that marred my bliss during sex with Jack was the fear of becoming pregnant. He didn't have a condom, and I hadn't been fitted with a coil or a diaphragm, either. But although he pulled out at the last moment, he didn't really hold back and afterward instructed me to get into the bathtub and make sure "to get as much of it out as you can."

Not the most romantic ending to my first night of love.

Now that Jack and I were having an affair, and the sizzling chemistry between us was so obvious, word of our illicit relationship traveled back to America so fast that it made my head spin. Within days, Rodgers and Hammerstein, set on smashing my love affair with Jack, ordered me home from Europe immediately, earlier than initially planned, to prepare for my next role in the movie of *Carousel*, in which I would play Julie Jordan, the star-crossed heroine who falls hopelessly in love with bad boy, carnival barker, Billy Bigelow. How could I say no?

Set in 1880 and based on Ferenc Molnár's 1909 play, *Liliom*, *Carousel* was a big hit on Broadway for Rodgers and Hammerstein. The story of rough, macho rogue Billy Bigelow, who at the start of the show has been dead for fifteen years but is given a chance by the "Starkeeper" to go back down to Earth one more time to try to redeem himself, was much beloved by audiences.

Long before I was finally cast as Julie in *Carousel*, the rumor mill had it that Judy Garland, fresh from her triumph in *A Star Is Born*, would be playing Julie instead. When I found out that she wasn't and that the role was mine, I was flattered, as Judy Garland had always been one of my idols.

When I eventually met Judy in the early sixties, I learned the hard lesson that sometimes it is better not to meet your heroes and heroines in the flesh. We were booked to appear on the same talk show together, and I was thrilled and excited at the prospect of meeting the one and only Judy Garland at last. We met backstage, and Judy drank glass after glass of wine.

I told her that I was a great fan of hers and admired her so much, but instead of responding graciously, she just took another glass of wine and walked over to the window.

"When in hell are they going to put us on!" she complained, impatient and irritated at having to wait for her cue. Although I didn't know it at the time, she was at the tragic end of her life, and in her own world, due to drugs. She died soon after.

Back in 1956, though, with Judy Garland out of the picture, the part of Julie in *Carousel* was well and truly mine, and *Carousel* and its beautiful score, which included "If I Loved You" and "You'll Never Walk Alone," was to become my all-time favorite musical.

At the time, another, less well-known song from *Carousel* resonated with me deeply. "What's the Use of Wond'rin'?" is Julie's lyrical answer to her friends' warning her about Billy. The song included the line "What's the use of wond'rin' if he's good or if he's bad?" and ended with "He's your fella and you love him. There's nothing more to say."

All of which encapsulated the essence of all my many conversations with Sari and my other friends who continued to warn me about Jack, that he was married and a philanderer, and that he would ultimately break my heart. I listened, but to paraphrase the song, Jack was my fella, I loved him, and there was nothing more for me to say.

For the time being, however, Jack and I were destined to be apart. *Carousel* was scheduled to shoot in Boothbay Harbor, Maine, and he was all set to appear as Leonard Vole in Agatha Christie's *Witness for the Prosecution*, in Bucks County Playhouse.

During our three-month separation, he would call me every night, and all day long I would look forward to his call. Whenever he could, he came up to Maine to visit me. When, at last, we were reunited after *Carousel* wrapped, he gave me the wonderful news that he and Evelyn had gone to Mexico and obtained a divorce, and that he was now free to marry me. His Parisian promise had not been a lie, after all, and I was overjoyed.

Before flying up to Boothbay Harbor, I spent eight weeks at Twentieth Century Fox, in Hollywood, rehearsing for *Carousel* with my costar, Frank Sinatra, and recording all the beautiful songs from the score, together.

From the first, Frank, fresh from his triumph in *From Here to Eternity*, made it clear that he was so thrilled about starring in *Carousel* and kept telling me that Billy Bigelow was the best role for a male singer there is. So I didn't have any qualms about accepting when one of his gofers approached me after rehearsals one day and asked me to stop by Frank's dressing room.

When I got there, the room was empty. I was about to leave when Frank shouted out from the bathroom, "I'll be right out." In a couple of minutes, he appeared, dressed only in slacks, bare-chested, with a towel slung around his neck. The prelude to a pass? Maybe.

The prospect of Frank's making a pass didn't bother me because I was never afraid of men wanting to pressure me into going to bed with them. For me, the decision was always mine, and mine alone. In Frank's case, that decision was a firm and resounding no!

My passion for Jack was one reason for my immunity to Frank Sinatra's fabled charms. But even if Jack hadn't been in the picture, I would never have gone to bed with Frank. Sure, I admired his voice, but as a man, he had no magic whatsoever for me. He was so self-involved, and every single conversation centered only around him and no one else.

He was also massively insecure. I remember going backstage after one of his concerts years later and telling him how brilliant he'd been.

"Nah, that last note in my third song? I didn't make it," Frank said.

"But, Frank, you were fine."

"Nah, Shirley, I'm gonna go home." And he did.

Anyway, at my meeting alone with Frank during the *Carousel* rehearsals, for a while he prowled around the dressing room in silence. He stared at me out of the corner of his legendary blue eyes. Striking as those eyes were, I felt decidedly uncomfortable under their stare.

Finally, Frank said, "I think this is going to be a terrific picture, don't you?"

I nodded.

"I think we ought to rehearse together as much as we can, and make the best movie we can."

I nodded again.

Then Frank sat down on the couch next to me. "You're a beautiful girl and a beautiful singer."

Here it comes, I thought to myself, because Frank had a reputation of going to bed with every leading lady he ever worked with.

He leaned closer to me. "I really want to talk to you about this role, who we are, what the script really means," he said earnestly.

So Frank really did want to talk about *Carousel* and wasn't going to make a move on me! I breathed a sigh of relief.

As he knew that I had worked with Rodgers and Hammerstein on *Oklahoma!* and was under contract to them, he asked me all about them. He quizzed me on how they felt about *Carousel*, why it was their favorite of all their musicals, and their plans for the movie.

When I left Frank's dressing room a while later, I was full of admiration for his dedication to playing the part of Billy Bigelow and to making *Carousel* a giant success.

After we'd finished rehearsing in the studio, I traveled up to Boothbay Harbor ahead of Frank and fell in love with the town at first sight. I had my little cabin on the water and, with my love of nature and animals, was in heaven. I'd grown up in a small country town with cows and horses roaming around, and Boothbay Harbor was so darling, so familiar, so much my kind of place, and I was so happy there. It only remained for Frank to arrive so that we could start shooting *Carousel* together.

All of us, including Frank, had been told beforehand that some of the *Carousel* scenes had to be shot twice because of the complexities of the new process, CinemaScope 55, which would help guarantee the movie's success. We all knew that the new system was a crowd-pleaser and were happy to go along with whatever it took.

On the first day of shooting, we were scheduled to shoot the first scene between Frank and me. I was on set, waiting for Frank to arrive, when his limo pulled up. Frank got out of the limo and took one look at the two lots of different cameras already in position. "I signed to do one movie, not two," he growled, then got right back into his limo and ordered the driver to take him straight back to the airport. Frank had walked out on *Carousel* on the very first day of filming.

Producer Henry Ephron (whose first shot as a producer was this, after a distinguished career as a screenwriter and playwright) was on the set and witnessed what happened. With tears rolling down his cheeks, he came over to me and asked if I knew where Gordon MacRae, my wonderful *Oklahoma!* costar, was. I told him Gordon was in Tahoe, doing his nightclub act. Can you get ahold of him? Ephron asked, and handed me a bunch of quarters.

From a pay phone by the water, I called the Tahoe hotel where Gordon was performing, got him on the phone, and asked him point-blank if he would like to play Billy Bigelow in *Carousel*.

Gordon didn't pause for even a second. "Give me three days. I gotta lose ten pounds."

And after a three-day diet of half a grapefruit and an egg, three times a day, and nothing else, Gordon lost ten pounds, then signed to play Billy Bigelow in *Carousel*.

Gordon had saved the day and I was glad, but I still couldn't quiet the little voice inside my head that kept asking over and over why Frank Sinatra had quit a role he so desperately longed to play in a movie that he wanted to be in so much.

The official answer was that "one-take Frank," as he was known in the business, wasn't prepared to do two takes for *Carousel*. But he had known way ahead of time that *Carousel* would be filmed twice for CinemaScope 55. So why did he balk when he saw two lots of cameras on the set and then walk out without another word?

Through the years, whenever I saw Frank, I tried over and over to get him to answer that question, but with no luck. Every time I broached the subject, he would bristle and say, "Drop it, Shirl!"

On February 14, 1958, I appeared on Frank's show with him, and in a moment replete with irony we sang the duet "If I Loved You," the romantic ballad from *Carousel*, the song that we would have sung in the movie together.

I saw Frank for the last time toward the end of his life at a benefit. He was called up onstage but was so frail that he had to have someone help him up the stairs. Once he got to the microphone, he started to speak, then said, "To hell with this, I can't get anything out right now!" and turned around and walked off again. As he was coming down the stairs, he gave a nod in my direction and said, "Hiya, Shirl, how ya doing?"

I smiled at him. He died shortly afterward, without ever telling me the real reason he walked out on *Carousel*.

I finally found out the truth a few years ago, when I was at a press conference and an old-time journalist at the back of the room yelled out to me, "Hey, Shirley, do you know the real reason Frank left *Carousel*?"

"Sure," I said confidently. "He had a big thing about not doing the same scene twice. He only ever did one take and was proud of it."

"No, Shirl, that wasn't the real reason."

According to the journalist, at the time Frank was due to start filming *Carousel*, his grand passion, Ava Gardner, was shooting another film and was getting lonesome for Frank.

She called him and, according to the journalist, said, "You better get your ass down here, Frankie, otherwise I'm going to have an affair with my costar."

Poor Frank didn't know that another actress on the shoot was already having an affair with the costar, and that Ava was making an empty threat to Frank.

But because Ava was his dream girl, the woman he would love for the rest of his life, Frank dropped everything, walked out of *Carousel*, and flew to be with Ava, to prevent her from having an affair she probably wasn't going to have anyway. Mystery solved. Part of me felt sorry for Frank and understood why he dropped everything for Ava. And I did love his singing.

A footnote to my Frank Sinatra recollections: When I appeared on his show, I rehearsed beforehand with Nelson Riddle, and Nelson asked me, "What key do you sing in, Shirley?"

"I don't know. I can't read music. But I'll sing it in whatever key Frank wants," I said, leaving Nelson shocked to the core that I couldn't read music.

In any event, when Frank sang "If I Loved You," he sang it with warmth, passion, and emotion. As far as I was concerned, Frank Sinatra was always a gentleman.

I never encountered Frank's rough-and-ready Rat Pack persona, but I did meet Sammy Davis Jr. down the line and learn more about what made him tick.

Sammy adored Frank. Frank was his mentor, and if ever a hotel wouldn't allow Sammy to stay there because he was African-American, Frank wouldn't stay at that hotel, either. When Sammy died, Frank did everything to help his widow, Altovise.

Long before that, in the sixties, I met Sammy when Jack took me over to his home in Beverly Hills one night. Lines of cocaine were laid out on every table, and porno was playing on all the TV screens throughout the house. I just wasn't interested. Drugs didn't interest me at all, nor, in those days, did porno. Jack did nothing to pressure me to stay, and we left together without taking cocaine or watching any porno.

Not to say that I was totally innocent as far as drugs were concerned. Around the same time, Jack and I were in bed together one night when he suddenly produced a capsule and said he wanted me to try it.

"It's really great," he said, "and particularly wonderful if you do it during sex."

Such was my trust in Jack that the next time we had sex, when he cracked open the capsule, I sniffed the drug amyl nitrite (also known as poppers) for the first time in my life. I couldn't help confessing to Jack that the effect was amazing and enhanced my orgasm immensely. From then on, whenever Jack could get some amyl nitrite, we used it together during sex and loved how it increased our enjoyment.

As for porno, one night during the late sixties, my idol Anthony Newley invited Jack and me to dinner with him and his wife, Joan Collins, at their Beverly Hills home. I was elated to be meeting Tony, whom I admired so much as a singer.

The evening started off with drinks. Tony, the perfect host, was funny and charming, and Joan, who was wearing a low-cut something or other, seemed like an interesting woman.

She didn't have a maid on call that night but, instead, had made dinner herself. I was most impressed that she served three different kinds of food so we would have a choice between chicken, fish, or steak. Her cooking was good, and we ate quite a lot.

Afterward, the four of us moved into the beautiful living room and lounged on a big couch while we all had after-dinner drinks and chatted about show business.

All of a sudden, Tony Newley got up and announced, "Right, we've got some porno movies. Why don't we all get naked and watch together?"

Although the rest of the invitation was unspoken, this was the era of *Bob & Carol & Ted & Alice*, and it was clear what Tony was leading up to—swinging.

Jack gave me a piercing look. "How do you feel about that, Shirley?"

I shook my head. "Not me."

To his credit, Jack said straight out, "My wife is a very beautiful and sexy woman, but she really isn't interested in anything like that. And, listen, guys, it's late for us."

And we left.

That was then. Now, though, although swinging has never appealed to me in the least, I have to admit that in recent years, my attitude toward watching porno movies has undergone a radical transformation.

To return to the Rat Pack once more: Everyone has always assumed that Frank Sinatra was the leader of the Rat Pack. But in reality, Dean Martin was the true leader. Dean dictated how a number should be done. Dean told me that now and again when Frank wanted to rehearse a number, Dean would say, "Nah, I want to go and play a round of golf," and that's what he'd do instead. Then he just turned up for the show and performed his part in the act his way, with no rehearsal. He did drink, of course, but not during a show. Drinking onstage was just part of his act.

When Frank said at the very end that he wanted to take the Rat Pack show on the road one more time, Dean said, "I don't want to go on the road again. I'm outta here," and the Rat Pack never appeared onstage again.

I adored Dean Martin, appeared on his show four times, and thought he was great. He was so spontaneous. He never rehearsed anything. If I had to do a song with him, he would go through it a couple of times, and that would be that.

Dean and I were fond of each other, and we were neighbors in Bel Air. I always took my kids to the Hamburger Hamlet on Sunset Boulevard, and when Dean was no longer performing, that became his hangout as well, and I always used to see him there.

One night, Marty and I had dinner in the back room of the Hamburger Hamlet. When we came out to get our car, Dean was sitting at the bar, alone, watching TV. His teeth were out, he was munching spaghetti, and he was drunk.

He saw us and said, "Hi, Shirl, howya doing, honey?" and we chatted for a minute or two. I glanced out the window and noticed that his white Rolls-Royce was parked outside, but that he didn't have a driver waiting for him in it.

So I said, "Listen, Dean, why don't you let me and Marty drive you home?"

He shook his head. "Nah, I'll be fine."

"You've been drinking," I said as gently as possible.

"Don't be silly, Shirley. I know what I'm doing.

I'm gonna drive myself home. I do it all the time."

I gave him a kiss on the cheek, and Marty and I left.

Soon after, Dean was dead.

Was Dean Martin an alcoholic? I don't know. Whatever the truth, it isn't my way to be judgmental. After all, I'm the daughter of a brewer, and I do like my martini every afternoon at five. But that's it. In fact, Marty and I won a major lawsuit in the eighties after the *National Enquirer* claimed he had driven me to drink! Their story claimed that I was drunk by three every afternoon. The entire cast and crew of *The Partridge Family* confirmed that was not the truth, and Marty and I won the lawsuit.

We deserved our victory, but I do know all about drink and drinking. First, because of the family business, and all those hours I spent as a child playing pool and pinball in bars, then because I was married to Jack (who introduced me to drinking), and also because one of my favorite parts was playing an alcoholic Sunshine Girl in the *Playhouse 90* production "The Big Slide," with former circus clown and vaudeville comic Red Skelton.

"The Big Slide" was set in the 1920s. Red played Buddy McCoy, a down-on-his-luck comedian, and I played May Marley, the alcoholic Sunshine Girl who sings and dances in musicals. As my character committed suicide at the end of the play, the role gave me the chance to flex my muscles as a dramatic actress.

I only got the part through a stroke of luck. During rehearsals for "You're the Top: A Salute to Cole Porter," which would air on October 6, 1956, I was singing the iconic song "I Hate Men," from *Kiss Me, Kate,* and the director of "The Big Slide" happened to be in the studio and saw my performance, which was really down and dirty. Which is how I got cast against type in "The Big Slide."

As "The Big Slide" was to go out on live TV, the entire company rehearsed beforehand for five weeks, just as if we were preparing to put on a play in the theater. During rehearsals, I got to know Red Skelton pretty well and made the surprising discovery that his sense of humor was bluer than blue!

By another stroke of luck, when the play aired on November 8, 1956, my idol Burt Lancaster saw my performance and, as a result, offered me the part of Lulu Bains in *Elmer Gantry,* the part that would change my career, if not my life.

FIVE

If He's Good or If He's Bad

Carousel opened on February 16, 1956, to rave reviews, although it didn't turn out to be as big a box-office success as *Oklahoma!*—probably due to the darker subject matter of the plot.

My life, in contrast, was full of light. Jack and I got married at the Protestant Church of New Jerusalem in Cambridge, Massachusetts, at two in the afternoon of August 6, 1956, then four hours later, we performed the evening show of John Gay's *The Beggar's Opera* at the Sanders Theatre on the Harvard campus. During which we got married for a second time that day, onstage, as our characters, highwayman MacHeath and his paramour, Polly Peachum!

My childhood friend from Smithton, Red, was at our wedding, and so was Barbara Ruick, my costar from *Carousel*, along with Jack's parents and mine. Luckily, my father liked Jack a lot, but my mother did not and made no bones about how she thought he was the wrong man for me. She never minced her words and told Jack to his face how she felt about him. He just laughed. But she was convinced that he was an incorrigible ladies' man, and anytime she saw him through the years, she would always confront him about his womanizing.

"So, Jack, how many other women are you seeing on the side?" she'd ask.

"None, but don't worry, Marge, I'll soon find a few," Jack would retort, cool as a cucumber.

On our wedding day, after the show, in which Jack played the villainous MacHeath to perfection, we had a reception at the Ritz, where we were staying, then Jack and I retired to our suite.

We'd long been lovers, but I wanted my wedding night to be special. My trousseau, I decided, should not be white, given that I was no longer a virgin. Instead, I made up my mind that on this special night, I would transform myself into the ultimate vamp. I purchased a sheer, black lace baby-doll outfit, with black satin high heels. Funny wedding night.

After I laid it all out on our bed, I slipped into the bathroom to freshen up. When I came out, Jack was dressed in my outfit, complete with high heels. Then the doorbell rang, and there was my agent, Gus Schirmer, with a bottle of champagne in hand. When he saw Jack, the look on Gus's face was priceless. We all fell about laughing, and Gus had champagne with us, then left so that Jack and I could finally celebrate our union and make love as husband and wife at last.

• • •

August 6, 1956, wasn't just our wedding day. That day the *New York Times* announced that Gordon MacRae and I would star in "You're the Top," a ninety-minute CBS tribute to Cole Porter in October, which turned out to be the show that indirectly led to my fateful appearance in *Playhouse 90*'s "The Big Slide."

Cole Porter gave Jack his first big break on Broadway. Soon after our wedding night, Jack told me exactly what motivated Cole to hire an inexperienced sixteen-year-old from Jamaica, Queens, to dance in the chorus of his sophisticated Broadway show.

Despite the years that have passed, I remember Jack's story word for word. Most women who married a handsome man and assumed that they were going to live happily ever after with him, but then heard the story I heard from Jack, would probably remember it word for word as well.

Me: "So, Jack, did you ever meet Cole Porter?"

Jack: "Meet him! I had sex with him."

Me (after I'd picked myself up off the floor): "You did?"

Jack: "He was about to cast a new show. I wanted a job in it, and that was the way to get it. Somehow, someone invited me up for drinks at Cole Porter's apartment at the Waldorf, and then everybody left and I was alone with Cole."

Me (holding my breath): . . .

Jack: "I told a few funny stories, probably flirted with him some. Then the conversation stopped, and I took my penis out and said, 'Do you want some of this?' "

Jack's endowment was so vast, so desirable, that I had no doubt whatsoever about Cole Porter's answer.

I was shocked, but not dreadfully, when Jack said straight out, "I'm not gay, but if I need a job, I'll do whatever it takes to get it."

For whatever reason, partly because I loved him so much and for me he could do no wrong, and partly because my career had evolved so quickly, so easily, and so painlessly and it had not been that way for Jack, I understood.

In a way, I was happy that Jack had told me the truth. I didn't want him to keep anything from me. Besides, I didn't want to hear about Jack and Cole Porter from anyone else.

But when I read Gerald Clarke's biography *Truman Capote*, based on his interviews with Truman, I got a much more negative slant on the Cole Porter story than the version Jack presented me with.

Clarke quotes Capote as revealing, "There was another story Cole told me that I didn't use because it sounded rather unpleasant and I liked Cole. It was about his long affair with that actor, Jack Cassidy."

Long affair? Jack didn't give me the impression

that he had more than a one-evening encounter with Cole.

According to Clarke, Jack was uncharacteristically cruel to Cole, and I still have difficulty in believing the following story Capote claimed Cole Porter had told him:

"Cassidy would say, 'Do you want this cock? Then come and get it.'

"Then he would stand away so that Cole, whose legs had been paralyzed in that awful riding accident, would have to crawl toward him. Every time Cole got near, Cassidy would move further away. This went on for half an hour or forty-five minutes before Cassidy would finally stop and let Cole have it."

Difficult as it is for me to accept the possibility of truth in Capote's anecdote, I do know that Jack did have a dark side.

When he was young, he didn't want to go into the army, so on the application, he said he was gay, which meant that the army didn't take him. That story shocked and disappointed me.

Jack would never have labeled himself as bisexual, but I do know that he had had sex with men. When he was touring, he told me he roomed with various gay guys. I never questioned him about how many gay guys he'd had sex with. I didn't want to know. Ignorance is bliss, as they say.

He and director/choreographer Bob Fosse, creator of *Sweet Charity*, *Cabaret*, and *Chicago*, lived together on the road, but I don't think they had an affair with each other. Fosse was a notorious womanizer, and I do know from Jack that he and Fosse often had threesomes with women. Jack, Bob, and a woman.

In the seventies, when sexual promiscuity was the order of the day for many people, Jack did try to get me into a foursome with the handsome actor Pete Duel, who was just thirty years old, and Pete's girlfriend. Pete and Jack met when Jack appeared on the TV series *Alias Smith and Jones*, in which Pete played Joshua Smith. They became close and had plans to star in a play together.

Jack and I were living in Bel Air at the time, and Pete and his girlfriend came over for a swim party. We were all in the pool when Jack said, "Hey, let's all take off our clothes and go inside and have a foursome!"

I got out of the pool at once and said to Jack, "You go ahead, but I think I'll forgo this."

Then I went into the living room. After a few moments, Pete Deuel came in, put his arms around me, and said, "You know something, you're a very special lady."

"I'm sorry, I know that people do this, but it isn't something I want to get involved in."

He said, "I admire you for that."

And that was it.

Pete Duel was nice, and I was sad when he shot himself to death just a year later.

• • •

After Jack and I got married, our first apartment was on East Fifty-Second Street and the East River Drive in New York City. Jack was an incredible designer and loved to design both the interior of a room and the furniture in it. The décor had to be perfect for him to be happy. Sometimes, I felt that I wasn't perfect enough for him, either. He wanted me to be sophisticated, a woman of the world, a party giver of distinction, a great hostess. At least, half of him did, but I knew deep down that he would have resented it bitterly had I ever well and truly upstaged him. Jack wanted me to remain the small-town girl he'd met and married and who always ceded the spotlight to him.

So I followed my instincts, and although I learned to paint, to read more, to enjoy serious plays at the theater, all to please Jack, I made sure that when I was with him, I always stayed in the background. When we were socializing with other people, I'd spend most of the evening sitting quietly on a chair in the corner, not saying a word and living up to Jack's nickname for me of Mouse.

Soon after Jack and I were married, I got pregnant. My manager, Ruth Aarons, was horrified, and so was Jack. Ruth represented Celeste Holm, George Chakiris, Janis Paige, and Jack and me. Jack adored Ruth and followed her advice unquestioningly. So, up till then, did I. Now she and Jack were in unison, telling me that I had no alternative but to abort my unborn baby. Both of them said that my career was on the upswing and having a baby right now would be a disaster for it.

Abortion was illegal in those days, and I went through a great deal of soul-searching before agreeing to one. But Ruth was adamant. Having a child would end my career once and for all. So, against all my better instincts, and much against my will, I agreed.

Relieved, Ruth volunteered, "We have a doctor. . . ."

I had the sense that I wasn't the first of Ruth's illustrious clients to pay a visit to this doctor. Which didn't make me feel any better, but at least he wasn't a backstreet butcher.

Jack took me to the doctor's office in an unprepossessing downtown-Manhattan building, but was not permitted to stay and wait for me while I had the abortion. I was nervous, but the doctor was kind and made me feel at ease. He gave me some type of local anesthetic, and I watched him as he worked, finally removing a mass of blood, but no fetus, as it was too early for one to have formed inside me.

When it was all over, the doctor told me I was healthy and would be fine, but to go home, put my feet up, and rest. Jack came to pick me up and was warm, loving, and kind and said, "I am so sorry you had to go through this, but Ruth was right that this is the wrong time for you to have a child. But I know you want a child, and we'll have one. More than one."

His words were comforting, but nevertheless I still felt emotionally fragile, shell-shocked, and I vowed that I would never have another abortion in my life. I made a solemn promise to myself that as soon as I could, I would get pregnant again and have a family.

In the meantime, I had Jack's son by Evelyn Ward to contend with, seven-year-old David Cassidy.

Although Jack's marriage to Evelyn was on the rocks when he and I met, Evelyn loved Jack, she was devastated that he no longer loved her, and didn't intend to let him go easily. After she finally agreed to give him a Mexican divorce and then discovered that he was set on marrying me immediately, she was intent on getting revenge on us.

During our wedding rehearsal, she called Jack and said that he needed to speak to his son. Then she put David on the phone, and David (who had obviously been coached by his mother) said, "What are you doing, Daddy? Why are you marrying someone else?"

Jack was too shocked to answer David, so he said a few words to him about something else, then hung up. Evelyn wanted to make Jack feel dreadful just before his wedding, and she succeeded.

The night before our wedding, Evelyn called Jack again, claiming that David was hysterical that his father was marrying me and demanding that Jack fly down to New Jersey and explain himself to David, in person.

Jack felt terrible, but not only were we getting married, he had a show to do that night. However guilty he felt about David, he still stood up to Evelyn and said, "I will not, I cannot, leave now. You are going to have to handle this. You have to help David come to terms with the fact that I am marrying someone else."

After Jack refused to leave me and fly to New Jersey and talk to David in person, Evelyn made damn sure that he and I didn't sail into our new life without suffering. After all, she blamed me for the demise of her marriage to Jack. But I knew the truth. Even though Evelyn viewed me as the scarlet lady who had broken up her supposedly idyllic marriage to Jack, I knew that wasn't the case. By the time I met Jack, she and Jack had already been separated twice and then got back together again. After that, though, their marriage remained rocky.

After Jack divorced Evelyn, he paid her alimony and supported David, as well, but then stopped paying the alimony once Evelyn remarried. By that time, my career was doing extremely well, and as a result Evelyn took Jack to court in an attempt to increase David's child support. I didn't think she was wrong. I was compelled to take the witness stand and give evidence about my income, and she lost her case.

Evelyn's bitterness at losing Jack was at its height at the time of our wedding, although our court battle with her lay ahead of us. Nonetheless, for all the right and proper reasons, soon after our wedding Jack arranged for me to meet David for the first time. Beforehand, we were both aware that Evelyn had done her best to paint me to him as the wicked stepmother, the villainess of the world. Moreover, when David was just a little kid, she had told him all about Jack's philandering, and he was hurt and puzzled by his father's attitude toward his mother and his marriage to me.

In a worthy but misguided attempt to prepare David for meeting me, to soften his attitude toward me, Jack took David to see me in *Oklahoma!* But after seeing me on-screen, David still viewed me as a wicked stepmother, and I didn't blame him. So the prospect of meeting David Cassidy, my newly acquired stepson, was daunting to me in the extreme.

I don't think Jack had bothered to get to know David properly until David was about seven years old and stayed with us for the first time. He was shy and sat in the corner and never said a word. But he adored his father. The first time he ever went to see Jack in the theater, David was just three and a half years old, and the show was *Wish*

You Were Here, on Broadway. When Jack strode onstage, little David proudly piped up, "That's my daddy!"

In the taxi taking David, Jack, and Evelyn (to whom Jack was still married) back home from the theater, David, his eyes still shining, looked up at Jack and Evelyn and said, "When I grow up, I want to do what you do, Daddy." Jack and Evelyn both exchanged glances and said to David, "Only if you get through high school first."

David worshipped Jack. Everything Jack did, everything Jack liked, David ached to follow suit. If Jack loved a show, David wanted to see it. Jack would sing in front of him constantly, and David was overwhelmed by Jack's talent and wanted to be like him. David was thrilled to watch Jack perform, to hear him sing, and always said, "That's what I want to be."

David was a good child and always did everything Jack asked of him. But as obedient as he was, he still couldn't measure up to the image of the perfect child that Jack expected him to be.

When the day of our proposed meeting arrived, Jack had taken care to plan every detail. He arranged for David to come and spend the night at our apartment, then intended that both of us take David to the movies the next day.

David arrived, and I was immediately struck by what a beautiful child he was, but also by how very much of a lonely only child he seemed to be. Gorgeous-looking, but quiet and clearly scared to death by meeting me. Naturally, he resented me deeply and felt that I had taken his father away from his mother. I can understand his thinking that, but it wasn't the truth. The marriage was long over before I arrived on the scene.

But David was now my stepson, he was sweet, adorable, and I was keen to win him over, so I sat down on the couch in our living room, patted the seat next to me, and said, "Come and sit next to me, David, let's talk."

He shook his head.

Jack was livid.

I took him aside. "Look, Jack, it's the first time David has met me. We need to be patient and understanding with him. Because he isn't a bit happy to be here."

Jack didn't have any patience with children. He wanted to be a child himself and to be the center of attention at all times.

"Well, he'd better get happy," he said, which hindsight would later prove to be a telling phrase.

We took David out to dinner, but he didn't want to go to the movies the next day. All he wanted to do was go home, so Jack relented and drove him home to New Jersey, where he lived with Evelyn.

I felt dreadful and as if David had hated me from the moment he met me. Only years later did I find out that he hadn't hated me at all. He generously said of me, "The first time I met her, I was six or seven and not impressed with whether she was famous. I wanted to hate her, but in minutes warmed to her."

At the time, though, David didn't want to be around me, and I understood and accepted his emotions wholeheartedly. Jack, however, did not and would continually ask me to take David to the park. But David would always refuse because he still blamed me for Jack's having divorced David's mother. And his mother continued to fuel the flames of his negative feelings about me.

When I became David's stepmother, he didn't talk to me much at all. We were both acutely aware that his mother was his mother, and I was not.

I left David alone with Jack most of the time and didn't push him to relate to me. I knew that pushing him wouldn't work. He had to come round to me. I didn't have to come round to him. But by the time he was nine, he was talking to me more, asking me questions about show business, what it was like to get onstage and sing, what it was like making movies. I first heard him sing when he was ten and got his first guitar. It was obvious to me even then that David was a natural.

Most of the time, as a child, he was with Jack and not with me. But I never felt left out as I wasn't around a lot and was usually away on location in such places as Rome, Lisbon, and South America. If I was around, I was always acutely aware that David was Jack's child, and I didn't try to exert any influence on him. I just didn't feel that was my role. I also felt it wasn't my place to intervene between David and Jack. Now and again Jack would ask my opinion about David, particularly when he was in his teens and wanted to go to a club with a girl, and I would give Jack my opinion. Sometimes Jack would follow my advice, other times not.

If anyone had compelled me to judge Jack's parenting skills during those years, I'd have been forced to admit that he was never much of a father. He never went to any of David's Little League games, after promising he would attend. To Jack, one phone call telling David, "I'll be there in spirit," took care of any obligation to be there in reality. Jack neglected David shamefully and, down the line, would do the same to our three sons together, Shaun, Patrick, and Ryan.

I believe, though, that Jack hurt David far more than he hurt Shaun, Patrick, and Ryan. When David was nine or so, I'd often see him crying in the corner because of something Jack had said or done to him, and I did my best to comfort him. That didn't stop Jack from playing the heavy father and disciplining David far too much, sometimes even paddling him, just as my mother did to me and Jack's mother did to him. As a result, David became afraid of Jack, and I didn't blame him at all.

However, I always nursed the fond hope that David would get to know Jack and the two of them would become closer to each other. One time, when David was twelve, I convinced Jack to go with him on a camping trip in the San Bernardino Mountains, where they were scheduled to stay at a Boy Scouts camp together. Only with Jack being Jack, he and David had little togetherness on that trip.

When David and all the other kids were fast asleep, Jack, who'd brought some Scotch along with him, sat around the campfire and regaled the other dads with his showbiz stories and his standard repertoire of jokes.

In the morning, poor David was practically mobbed by all the other fathers eager to praise Jack for his wit, charm, and bonhomie. As always, Jack was the center of attention, just the way he liked it, and David was overshadowed utterly and completely.

Later on, Jack started taking David with him when he went on summer-stock tours, and David, at last, had a chance to get to know his father better.

However, David never lived with us until the summer of 1968, when Jack and I rented a hundred-year-old stone castle, which boasted turrets and stained-glass windows, in Irvington-on-Hudson, while we were rehearsing for the Broadway show *Maggie Flynn*.

David came to live with us, and during that time he became closer to his brothers, Shaun, Patrick, and Ryan. When Shaun was born, I had been worried that David would feel left out and be jealous and vindictive toward Shaun, but David turned out to be quite the reverse. David and Shaun never had any sibling rivalry, partly because David was so much older than Shaun, and later on, as Shaun grew older, he looked up to David. Although David lived with his mother in West Orange, New Jersey, whenever he came to visit us, the boys always loved seeing him and vice versa. I think he was happy to be part of a big family.

David was good-natured and threw himself into playing with Shaun, and later Patrick and Ryan, taking them swimming and riding bicycles with them. David loved to babysit the boys and was extremely responsible when he did.

The boys particularly enjoyed the pillow fights they often had with David. If David ever tired of playing with his brothers, who were so much younger than him (Shaun was eight years his junior; Patrick, twelve years; and Ryan, sixteen), he could always escape to the pool house, where he sometimes entertained young ladies.

Ladies, girls, women, had always been a part of David's life. Like his father, he was highly sexed, and in his autobiography he confessed that he had his first sexual experience when he was nine years old and fondled a friend's sister. So even as a young boy, he played the field with girls. Throughout his early teens, women flocked to him in droves. Although I never met any of them in person, I was constantly aware that David had girlfriends everywhere, but nothing serious. Jack also knew how numerous these girls were and would sometimes crossly complain, "That's all he cares about, girls."

Whereupon I would laugh and say, "Well, Jack, he's your son, and that's all you care about."

David also had something else in common with Jack: a giant endowment. David's brothers called him Donk, for Donkey, and Jack would joke, "Where did you get that? You're bigger than me," which probably didn't help their rocky relationship.

SIX

Elmer Gantry

By now, all the Hollywood power players viewed me as the ingénue from *Oklahoma!* and from *Carousel* and didn't consider me to be anything other than a singer who starred in musicals.

That infuriated me—I was an actress, and I wanted nothing more than to act in a serious drama and to be taken seriously. In the meantime, when Jack wasn't starring on Broadway, he and I performed our cabaret act all over the country together.

We were about to go onstage at the Fairmont Hotel in San Francisco to do our act when the phone rang.

"This is Burt Lancaster," a deep male voice announced.

Burt Lancaster! Burt Lancaster! My teen idol. Must be a joke, I thought, and hung up.

Within seconds, it rang again. It really was Burt Lancaster. Burt Lancaster, only not making a social call.

"This is Burt Lancaster. Have you read the novel *Elmer Gantry*?"

I hadn't.

"Go get it and read it. We're making a movie of it, and I would like you to think about playing the role of Lulu Bains. Can you come in and meet Richard Brooks, who is directing?"

Sure I could.

Overnight, I read the book and discovered that Lulu Bains wasn't Laurey or Julie or some musical ingénue but a real, flesh-and-blood woman, the daughter of a deacon, undone by passion and forced into prostitution.

Burt had seen me playing the alcoholic Sunshine Girl in "The Big Slide," a *Playhouse 90* television drama with Red Skelton, and had never forgotten me. But to play Lulu Bains in *Elmer Gantry*, I would first have to pass muster with the movie's fearsome writer, producer, director (all rolled into one), Richard Brooks.

Known for directing gritty, dramatic movies such as *Cat on a Hot Tin Roof* and *Blackboard Jungle*, Richard Brooks was universally reviled as a martinet. I also knew through the grapevine that he intended Piper Laurie (who had also played an alcoholic in another *Playhouse 90* production, "Days of Wine and Roses") to play the part of Lulu Bains.

Richard Brooks definitely did not want to cast me as Lulu Bains, and however much Burt Lancaster wanted me to play Lulu and was rooting for me, I was petrified at the prospect of meeting Richard Brooks.

But I also knew that this was my big opportunity to make the switch from frothy musicals to drama, to be considered a serious actress at last, and not just a singer. It all depended on my winning over Brooks, and I wasn't at all sure whether I was equal to the task.

I knew through other actresses and actors who had worked with Brooks that he was an ex-marine and a tough guy. Everyone who'd worked for him on movies hated him. He didn't allow anyone to play cards between scenes or to read newspapers. Famous for calling the cast and the crew "sons of bitches," he would think nothing of slapping an extra in the face if the extra was meant to cry in a scene but hadn't so far managed to wring out a single tear. One hard slap from Richard Brooks, and that same extra was wailing like a baby.

Down the line, in 1985, during the making of *Fever Pitch*, which Brooks was directing, he employed that identical tactic on my own son Patrick, who had a small part in the movie. Brooks wanted Patrick to cry in one scene, and as much as Patrick tried to cry on demand, he couldn't manage it. So even though Brooks was fully aware that Patrick was my son, he still slapped him in the face a few times—and with so much force that Patrick began crying.

While he was directing *Elmer Gantry*, Brooks went too far. He suddenly swore viciously at one of the crew. Outraged, the crew member took revenge on Brooks the next day, deliberately running his car over Brooks's foot. Brooks was rushed to the hospital, but even so, he didn't modify his treatment of his cast and crew one iota. That was the Richard Brooks who held my career in the palm of his muscular hands.

Burt Lancaster had prevailed on Brooks to meet me, so there I was one Saturday at the studio in Hollywood, after having flown down from San Francisco, where Jack and I were playing at the Fairmont.

I'll never forget that first harrowing interview with him. I wore a tight, white dress so that he could see my figure. He grilled me for an hour and a half. All the time, he was sprawled on a couch, his face turned away from me, while he sucked on his pipe and barked questions at me, which I attempted to answer to the best of my ability.

Then he handed me the pages of the script in which Lulu Bains was featured, as opposed to the script as a whole. Richard Brooks never allowed any of the actors in his movies to see the complete script, only the pages covering their part.

Fortunately, following Burt Lancaster's advice, I had already read the novel, by Sinclair Lewis, so I knew the story and my character. I went out in the corridor, read the pages Brooks had given me, then went in again and cleared my throat, expecting to start reading my part and auditioning.

Before I did, I made a speech to Richard Brooks, declaring my passion for *Elmer Gantry*: "I'd play the part for nothing, Mr. Brooks."

But instead of letting me read the script for him, Brooks waved me aside. "So do you think you could play Lulu?" he barked.

I said I thought I could.

Then he dismissed me. I went home in tears, convinced that Richard Brooks definitely didn't want me to play the part. My opinion was buttressed the following morning when word came back to me that Brooks hadn't thought much of me and had no intention of casting me in the role.

But Burt Lancaster wasn't giving in, and faced with his star power and persistence, Richard Brooks finally capitulated and the part was mine.

Knowing that I was far from the flavor du jour in the eyes of Richard Brooks, Burt strongly advised me to be on set from day one. As Brooks shot in sequence, and my scene came toward the end of the movie, I had ample opportunity to observe him directing. As I did, although I was hugely intimidated by him, he ultimately won my admiration. But that didn't mean he would reciprocate.

My first day of filming *Elmer Gantry* proved to be the biggest challenge of my career. Richard Brooks had personally chosen my costume: a slip that partially revealed my breasts, but not so much as to inflame the censors. I was extremely nervous, but due to Burt, I was also well prepared for the scene.

Through the years since I made *Elmer Gantry*, I've often been asked if I researched my part, as the deacon's daughter turned prostitute, by going to a house of prostitution and talking to the ladies there. I didn't think I needed to go that far. I knew all about prostitutes because Jack had introduced me to some of them, ex-girlfriends of his who had moved from prostitution to acting for a living. So by the time I was to shoot the first scene, which took place in a house of prostitution, I was primed to play my part.

Nonetheless, that first scene proved to be the hardest scene I've ever shot in my life. In that scene I tell the other prostitutes all about the traveling salesman turned evangelical minister Elmer Gantry, what he did to me, and how I came to be working in the house: "Oh, he gave me special instructions back of the pulpit. He got to howlin', 'Repent! Repent!' and I got to moanin', 'Save me! Save me!' and the first thing I know he rammed the fear of God in me so fast I never heard my old man's footsteps."

That line "rammed the fear of God into me so fast" would send shock waves through America when the movie was released. In many places, it was actually cut from the movie, and I received hundreds of letters from fans of *Oklahoma!* and

Carousel demanding to know how I dared play such a sinful character.

That first day on the set, Richard sat on the sidelines, with his legs crossed, smoking his pipe, and didn't say a single, solitary word to me or give me a moment's direction, except to growl, "Okay, let's see how you do it." And that was it.

Until then, I was accustomed to directors actually directing me, but Richard Brooks said nothing. Not a word. Nada. Neither before the scene or after it.

That night, I went home in tears, convinced that Richard Brooks hated me and that the very next morning I was going to be fired.

Then the telephone rang.

"Shirley, this is Richard Brooks. I owe you an apology. I just saw the dailies of the scene you did, and you were brilliant. You were great in that scene. And I predict that you are going to win the Academy Award."

From that moment on, Richard Brooks was in my corner, and I even went on to do another movie with him, *Happy Ending*, in which he cast me as a kept woman, a lady of easy virtue, which was how he would forever view me after Lulu Bains and *Elmer Gantry*.

In my second big scene in *Elmer Gantry*, Burt, now in character as a superstar minister, comes to see me and wants to give me money because he knows that I was once a nice girl who fell into prostitution because of him. He tries to hand me the money, and I finally take it and slide it into my stocking top.

Then he kisses me passionately—a wonderful experience for me, as Burt Lancaster was a world-class kisser, better than any actor who'd ever kissed me on camera before, and any actor who would kiss me on camera afterward.

During that scene, part of my reason for kissing Elmer Gantry is that I have arranged for a photographer to lurk outside my window to snatch a picture of the saintly Elmer Gantry kissing me, a prostitute.

Afterward, Jean Simmons, as the Aimee Semple McPherson character, Sister Sharon Falconer, comes to see me to pay me off. I do one of those big scornful laughs because I am not interested in the money, just the attention. That scene, and all the others to follow, were harrowing in the extreme.

British actress Jean Simmons, of *Guys and Dolls* and *The Robe*, was wonderful in the part of Sister Sharon Falconer, and I was shocked and disappointed when she failed to be nominated for the Best Actress Academy Award.

Until *Elmer Gantry*, I was seen as a musical star, not an actress. *Elmer Gantry* and Lulu Bains changed all that for me. I was nominated for the Academy Award for Best Actress in a Supporting Role but never dreamed that I would win. My competition was both stiff and stellar: Janet Leigh for *Psycho*, Shirley Knight for *The Dark at the Top of the Stairs*, Mary Ure for *Sons and Lovers*, and Glynis Johns for *The Sundowners*.

I was the dark horse in the Best Supporting Actress category, and I was so resigned to not winning that by the day of the ceremony—April 17, 1961—I hadn't even prepared an acceptance speech. Realizing that I hadn't, Jack wrote one for me in the limo, scribbling a few lines on a scrap of paper as we drew nearer to the Santa Monica Civic Auditorium, where the Academy Awards ceremony was being held that night.

I didn't think I had a chance of winning, but I was determined to enjoy the evening, and the beautiful gold-and-silver ball gown that Don Loper had designed for me specifically for the ceremony. It had a massive skirt, which Loper had created to hide my pregnancy.

Elizabeth Taylor sat just a few tables from ours, and she looked utterly stunning. Years later, when she was married to Richard Burton, she invited us to a fund-raiser in her home.

By the time we arrived, Richard was quite drunk, and when Elizabeth introduced me to him, he slurred, "Shirley Jones! You must be Welsh!"

"Yes, I am."

"No wonder you can sing like that then," Richard exclaimed. "Can you sing in Gaelic?"

I said I couldn't.

"Well, then, I'll teach you!" He grabbed me by the hand, pulled me into one of the bedrooms, and closed the door behind us.

Oh, no, I thought. *Here we go.*

But instead of making a pass at me, Richard started to sing heartily in Gaelic, then handed me a song sheet, exhorting, "Just practice it!"

"But, Richard, it's far too hard for me. I can't sing in Gaelic. I wasn't even born in Wales!"

Richard just laughed, and soon we were singing together at the top of our voices.

Then the door swung open, and there stood Elizabeth, fuming. "You get your ass out here, Richard. We have a few people who wanna say hello to you." She dragged him away. I am sure she was worried he was going to make a pass at me. Given his track record, she had every reason to be.

But back then, on April 17, 1961, when Elizabeth and I were both nominated for Academy Awards, Elizabeth for Best Actress for her performance in *Butterfield 8*, all of Hollywood was at our feet.

When Welsh actor Hugh Griffith (who won Best Supporting Actor the year before for his role in *Ben-Hur*) announced the winner as "Shirley . . ." in a drink-slurred voice, I thought he was going to say "Shirley Knight." Then I heard Jack's whoop of pleasure. And then he kissed me. I had won Best Supporting Actress at the Thirty-Third Academy Awards. In a dream, I got up onstage and recited the speech Jack had scribbled for me on that piece of paper:

Thank you very much. I can only think that I wouldn't be standing here tonight accepting this Oscar if it weren't for another Oscar—Hammerstein—and Mr. Richard Rodgers. And also for the belief of Mr. Burt Lancaster, Mr. Richard Brooks, and Mr. Bernie Smith, hiring me and allowing me to play the part of Lulu Bains in Elmer Gantry. *This is the proudest moment of my career because of them. Thank you all.*

That was, indeed, the proudest night of my career. But winning that Academy Award would prove to be the beginning of the end for my marriage to Jack.

When Jack and I first met, I was the ingénue, the Hollywood Cinderella; he was the big Broadway star and my Prince Charming. After I won the Academy Award, our roles reversed, and Jack started to exhibit marked jealousy of my success.

One night soon after I was nominated for the Oscar, after the premiere of Susan Hayward's movie *Back Street,* Jack and I were invited to a party at the home of Ross Hunter, who had produced it. Ross was a legendary producer who had resuscitated Lana Turner's career with *Imitation of Life*, had produced a slew of Doris Day/Rock Hudson movies, and would go on to produce *Airport* and *Lost Horizon.*

Toward the end of the night, Ross made the big mistake of asking me what it felt like being nominated for an Academy Award. Before I could answer, Jack stood up unsteadily, very much the worse for wear from drink.

"Lemme tell you all about it," he slurred. For some reason I never could figure out, he laced into Ross directly. "Show business is a lousy business today, Ross." Jack went into a drunken tirade. He had a point, but this clearly was neither the time nor the arena in which to make it. We were guests in Ross Hunter's home, his movie had just premiered, and Jack shouldn't have dominated the conversation like that.

Unperturbed, Ross waved to Jack to sit down and shut up, but Jack wasn't having any of it.

"Say hello to Norman Maine," Jack declared, alluding to the character played by James Mason in *A Star Is Born*, who was upstaged by his former-ingénue wife, played by Judy Garland.

Jack was joking, and everyone laughed. I didn't laugh, though. Jack's comment was far too close to the bone. I knew that he was having problems with my being the star, especially a star with an Academy Award nomination. I wasn't happy about the situation, either. Old-fashioned as this

131

may sound nowadays, I wanted Jack to be the star in the family, to be number one, to take over the room, to feel that he was the man of the house.

So from that time on, even more than I had before, I began to play myself down. I would always let Jack do all the talking whenever we were in company together. And like many other wives of unfaithful husbands, I began to assiduously turn a blind eye to his rampant infidelity. I believed I was in part to blame for his infidelity by being more successful than he was.

So-called friends would whisper to me, "Jack's leading lady is crazy about him and . . . ," but I never reacted. I never confronted Jack or asked him any questions. Instead, I pushed all thoughts of his infidelity right out of my mind. It wasn't difficult for me to adopt that tactic because I was so secure as a person and as a performer.

You could say that I opted to play ostrich and stick my head in the sand. Even though I had married Jack knowing that he was a womanizer, I had avoided thinking about whether he would be faithful to me. I knew he was a handsome, sexual man who liked women, and I figured that if he was inclined to be unfaithful, then that would happen, and I would just have to put up with it. I also passionately hoped that, somehow, he would be faithful to me anyway.

Looking back through the prism of the years, I still don't think I would have handled Jack's infidelity any differently. We had three boys, and although I had married the prince of my dreams, all these other would-be princesses were lurking about, desperate to snare him. And many did, at least for a short time each.

Sadly, I was not alone in marrying the love of my life, then discovering that he had sexual passions other than me. It was an age-old, all-too-common occurrence in marriages. In some ways, I coped with infidelity more easily than might most women. I had my own life, and many men were courting me. That I didn't succumb to them at that time in my life is another issue. But I did have options, even though I didn't take them. Despite knowing that Jack wasn't true to me, I never felt insecure or wanting, nor did I change anything about myself because, through it all, Jack still treated me as if I meant all the world to him.

His approach did change somewhat when we'd been married for about three years and he inexplicably started to be up-front about his infidelities, almost as if he wanted me to approve of them. He declared, "You do understand, Mouse, that when I'm out on the road for a long time, there is going to be a woman in my life? It won't mean anything, but I'm very sexual, and my infidelities won't take anything away from you in any shape or form. You are always going to be the love of my life, always."

"That doesn't make me happy" was all I could

muster, once I'd digested the enormity of Jack's words.

"I know, Mouse, but I want you to know that it doesn't mean a thing. That's just how I am," he went on blithely.

By that time, Shaun and Patrick were already born, I was more deeply in love with Jack than ever, and I guess I just put his infidelities to one side. I thought to myself, *If this is the man whom I married, and this is the way it is going to be, then I am going to have to accept it.* After that, the subject was closed, and neither Jack nor I ever raised it again.

Whenever I heard that he was having affairs all over town, I just lived with it. He was always discreet, and I never got anonymous phone calls or poison-pen letters rubbing my face in his infidelities.

I never caught him with another woman; I never doubted his love for me. I never asked myself why I wasn't enough for him. I was his wife, and that was enough for me. Besides, he was the father of my children, and he always came home to me in the end, so I was happy.

As the years went by, now and again other people did make allusions to Jack's womanizing ways. In 1971, he appeared with Bette Davis in the movie *Bunny O'Hare*, playing a police lieutenant, and soon after Bette and I were on *The Tonight Show* together.

Afterward, Bette took me aside and asked if I was still married to Jack Cassidy. I asked why she wanted to know, and she shook her head disapprovingly. "When I was making the movie with Jack, he said, 'Bette, just remember that I am going to get you into the goddamn bed before this movie is over.'"

I don't think Jack meant what he was saying to Bette. He was just teasing her. But if he wasn't, if he did try to get her into bed and succeeded, I didn't care. Jack loved me, and the more women he had, the less threatened I became. Just one woman, who was so special to Jack that he gave up all other women, however, would be quite a different story, one that would threaten me immeasurably, one I would one day be forced to grapple with.

Jack's infidelity was one negative aspect to our marriage, and his lack of parenting skills was another. I had to be both mother and father to the children. Jack was open about his being so much more interested in his career than in his sons. He would accept any theatrical job anywhere, even if it meant he would miss important events in the children's lives.

Whenever I was offered a movie that shot over Christmas, Thanksgiving, Easter, or the children's birthdays, I would stipulate in my contract that I had to have those days off. If the movie company refused to allow me those days off, I immediately turned down the job. Whenever possible, I took the children with me on location, along with their nanny, and I was content.

"He's yer feller and you love him," Oscar Hammerstein wrote, "and all the rest is talk." All in all, I loved Jack deeply, and that was all that counted for me.

SEVEN

The Music Man

The Music Man, the Broadway hit show by
Meredith Willson (who termed it "an Iowan's
attempt to pay tribute to his own state"), was to be
one of the last big Hollywood musicals ever
made. I'd seen the Broadway production, with
Robert Preston, for which he rightfully won a
Tony, and adored the musical. While I was still set
on consolidating my career as a dramatic actress,
I was delighted to be playing Marian Paroo, the
librarian who is, against her will, romantically
beguiled by charming con man, "Professor"
Harold Hill, who arrives in River City promising
to form a marching band with the boys there,
but who plans to abscond in the eleventh hour.

Marian, a truly liberated woman, was stern,
determined, but a romantic who, in the end, jettisons
all her principles and falls deeply in love with Hill.
The part was wonderful, and I had no intention of
losing it. Besides, Jack and I badly needed the
salary I'd be paid to star in *The Music Man*.

Initially, Jack L. Warner, the head of Warner Bros., decreed that Frank Sinatra should play Professor Harold Hill, but—in an exquisite irony, given Sinatra's past history in walking off *Carousel*—Meredith Willson, who created *The Music Man* and composed the score, decreed that unless Warner Bros. cast Robert Preston, who had played Professor Harold Hill on Broadway for two years to great acclaim and won a Tony for his bravura performance, there would be no movie.

Naturally, the autocratic Jack L. Warner—who firmly believed that Sinatra was a more bankable star than Preston—was determined to stick to his guns. To mollify Meredith Willson somewhat, Warner tried a different tack by approaching another major box-office star, Cary Grant, and inviting him to play Hill. Cary, to do him credit, disagreed, and informed Warner that no one other than Robert Preston should play Hill. Warner capitulated, and Preston won the part he had deserved all along.

A stellar cast was assembled, from eccentric British actress Hermione Gingold, who was cast as Eulalie Shinn, the wife of the irascible mayor, played by Paul Ford, to a young Ron Howard, who was cast as my little brother, Winthrop Paroo.

At first, I was slightly nervous about working with Robert Preston in *The Music Man*, as he'd been doing the show on Broadway for two years, with Barbara Cook as Marian. I was worried that he might cite Barbara and her brilliant performance in the show all the time: "But Barbara did this scene like that . . . ," and so on. But Bob was so great, so bighearted, that he never once mentioned the Broadway show or Barbara Cook to me. And his performance as Professor Harold Hill was consistently fresh and new.

Before we began, I started working on the dance numbers with *The Music Man*'s distinguished choreographer, Onna White.

Aware of her reputation and her talent, I came clean immediately: "I just have to tell you that I'm truly not a dancer."

She replied, "Honey, by the time we finish this movie, you are going to be the best damn dancer around."

One of the great joys of working on *The Music Man* was acting with seven-year-old Ronny Howard. He was shy and his father was always on the set, but Ronny was already a pro. He assumed the lisp manifested by his character, Winthrop, without the slightest problem and always knew his lines word perfect. He was adorable.

However, British actress Hermione Gingold, who made her Hollywood mark in *Gigi*, was not particularly pleasant to work with. She was aloof and spent most of the breaks in shooting sitting all by herself on the side of the set, ignoring everyone else. She didn't bother to get to know me at all, so that was that.

Some of the scenes were shot in Mason City, Iowa, which was Meredith Willson's hometown, on which he had based the fictional River City.

While filming, I made the shocking discovery that I was pregnant. For a while, I kept it a secret, in case the producers discovered it and fired me on the spot. Jack was out of work, and Marian the librarian was such a terrific part that I decided to hope for the best. Then, one day I realized that my pregnancy was becoming startlingly obvious. Shaun had been a ten-pound baby, and Patrick was clearly going to be the same. There was no way of hiding my pregnancy anymore.

So I invited Morton DaCosta, the director and producer of the movie, to have lunch with me. Morton had also produced and directed the movie *Auntie Mame*, with Rosalind Russell, and he went on to direct Jack and me in *Maggie Flynn* on Broadway. I told him the truth, knowing that too many of my scenes were already in the can for him to fire me from the movie.

When I gave him my news, Morton gulped, then decided that all would not be lost. From then on, he decreed, I was to be shot only from the waist up. I would also thenceforth be wearing a corset, and, if necessary, extra panels would be added to my dress so as to disguise my condition.

The costume department laced me up in tight corsets, tighter and tighter by the day, and the camera crew did shoot me from above the waist only, but that still didn't prevent my pregnancy from being an enormous problem when we were shooting the last scenes of the movie.

Robert Preston and I were standing on the footbridge, shooting the most romantic scene in *The Music Man*, in which he sang "Till There Was You" to me, and he was holding me extremely tight against his chest. As he kissed me passionately—the only kiss that took place between us during the movie—his eyes were closed. All of a sudden, the baby in my stomach gave an almighty kick!

Bob practically passed out in shock. Then he straightened up and gave me a quizzical look.

"That was Patrick Cassidy," I said by way of explanation, as I had already been told that my baby was a boy, and we had decided to call him Patrick, a lovely Irish name.

Years later, long after I made *The Music Man*, I assumed that Bob had recovered from being kicked in the stomach by my unborn child. He was appearing on Broadway, and Patrick, who had always been a great fan of his, went to see him.

After the show, Patrick went backstage and was escorted to Bob's dressing room. He held his hand out to Bob. "My name is Patrick Cassidy."

Robert Preston took three steps back. "Oh, no! We've already met."

Then he gave a big smile, and all was forgotten.

I was now an Academy Award winner for *Elmer Gantry*, and the star of one of the last blockbuster Hollywood musicals, *The Music Man*. While money wasn't exactly pouring in, by rights it shouldn't have been a problem.

But as always, Jack spent money as if it were going out of style. He decided, out of the blue, to remodel our house. As I said before, he was a talented interior designer and brilliant at designing and finishing furniture. So I kept silent while he built a workshop behind the house and started to design and build a sunroom, complete with barbecue and a poolroom.

In some ways, I was thankful that Jack was only remodeling the house, not insisting that we sell it and buy another one. His biggest dream was always to buy a farm in Vermont, perhaps as a second home, and I dreaded the day when he declared the time was ripe for us to start hunting for it. So I concluded that the workshop was a small mercy, although we couldn't afford it. Despite the fact that we often didn't have enough money to pay the bills, I continued to watch in silence as day after day the machinery Jack persisted in ordering was delivered, along with expensive furniture and antiques. If I ventured to broach the sore subject of our finances, he simply tuned me out. He didn't want to hear about it. You could say that both of us were adept at playing the same game: he didn't want to hear about my money worries, and I definitely didn't want to hear about his infidelities.

Until I made *Two Rode Together* in 1961 with Richard Widmark, the thought that I might retaliate for Jack's infidelity and have an affair myself never once occurred to me.

Sex was the furthest thing from my mind when I met the movie's director, John Ford, who was to win the distinction of becoming my all-time most unfavorite director, although I did admire his work on such movies as *Stagecoach*.

Before I met John Ford, I'd already heard through the grapevine that he wasn't a woman's director and that he believed women belonged in bed, that being their only value.

Apart from Ford's attitude toward women, the story of *Two Rode Together* wasn't particularly inspiring, and John Ford knew it, which didn't add to his mood during the shoot. The plot revolved round Jimmy Stewart, who played the partner in a saloon, and Richard Widmark, an army lieutenant who was helping my character (who went by the name of Marty Purcell) to find her younger brother, who had been kidnapped by Comanches.

The first day when I showed up on the set for *Two Rode Together*, in Brackettville, Texas, I discovered that my part was being totally rewritten, although it was just hours before the cameras were to start rolling.

Before we started shooting, I tentatively approached John Ford and asked him how he wanted me to wear my hair, and he just growled, "Do whatever you like, but just do it." He didn't give me any direction throughout the entire picture, and I thanked my lucky stars that I was working with Richard Widmark, who was kind and helpful to me, and a good actor, as his performances in *The Alamo* and *Judgment at Nuremberg* attest.

Aside from John Ford's marked lack of concern for me and the part I was playing, I was utterly thrown by the long white handkerchief that he had permanently hanging out of the corner of his mouth, as if he were chewing a straw or something. If ever he deigned to give one of us a direction, he'd yank the handkerchief out of his mouth, yell out a few instructions, then shove it back into his mouth again. By the end of the day, he had chewed it to shreds.

The first time I saw Ford chewing his handkerchief, I mouthed my shock at Richard Widmark. He shook his head, then leaned forward and whispered in my ear, "Just don't ask him, Shirley, don't ask him!"

So I bit my tongue and said nothing.

Thankfully, John Ford's lack of connection with me didn't mean that the shooting of *Two Rode Together* was to be wholeheartedly unpleasant for me. I was thrilled to be cast in this movie with Jimmy Stewart, as he was a good friend who was born and raised in Indiana, Pennsylvania, close to my hometown, Smithton.

From the first scenes, Jimmy was as helpful to me as he could be. Later on, when we worked together in *The Cheyenne Social Club*, for the only time in my career I dried up. Jimmy said, in his Jimmy Stewart style, "W-w-well, don't worry, Shirley, j-just say whatever comes into your head, and it will be p-p-perfect for the scene." I did, and he was right.

Jimmy Stewart was as endearingly funny and charming offscreen as he was on. In particular, he told me an adorable story about the birth of his twins, whom he worshipped at first sight.

Thrilled and excited to bring them home with his wife from the hospital, he raced there in his car, narrowly escaping a speeding fine from a watchful traffic warden. Arriving in front of the hospital, out of breath and overwhelmed, he parked his car and ran upstairs to his wife and the babies.

Jimmy wheeled his wife down to the lobby in a wheelchair and left her there, the twins in her arms, cooing happily. Then he went out to the car and promptly drove straight home, without them! He was so absentminded he had simply forgotten all about them!

His long-suffering wife later confided in me that this story was not an isolated incident. To describe Jimmy Stewart as befuddled and absentminded, it seemed, was the understatement of the year.

That first day on location for *Two Rode Together*, during a break in shooting Richard Widmark came over to me again, clearly feeling sorry for me because it was so obvious that John Ford had snubbed me. I didn't take it personally, though, as I knew how John felt about women in general.

Besides, I had two-year-old Shaun with me on location (along with his nanny), and that made me happy.

As shooting progressed, Richard Widmark made me happier still.

It all started out because Richard, who was then in his forties and was married to a playwright, had a car at his disposal while we were shooting the movie. So when we had some time off, he offered to show me the countryside. To my delight, I discovered that he loved nature as much as I did, and that he understood that I wasn't this sophisticated, dedicated actress, but was natural and adored the country.

So we'd set off in Richard's gray Ford and he would talk to me about the beauty of the country as we drove, rather like my father once had all those years ago when he drove me to Pittsburgh for my weekly singing lessons.

Soon, Richard stopped the car in a clearing and started kissing and hugging and touching me. Then he pulled away from me and said, "Don't worry, we are both married, and I'm not going to take advantage of you. You're twenty years younger than I am, you've got children, and I really care about you. But under different circumstances . . ."

We kissed again, then and often, in Richard's car, during our long country drives, and in his trailer, between shots. But I never went all the way with Richard. Despite Jack's infidelities, I still loved him, and I wanted to be true to my marriage vows. Richard understood.

On my seventieth birthday, Marty arranged for many of the stars with whom I'd worked to each create a congratulatory video message for me. So there was Richard Widmark, up on the screen, larger-than-life, giving me birthday wishes after all those years.

"Dear Shirley," he said, "happy birthday. Miss you a lot. We had such a good time together."

We certainly did.

When I made *The Courtship of Eddie's Father* in 1962, I was happy to be working with Ronny Howard again. He played Eddie, a little boy who was determined to find a wife for his newly widowed father. My character, Elizabeth Marten, ends up marrying his father, Glenn Ford.

Glenn was half-Welsh and had a prolific romantic track record, which encompassed, among others, Joan Crawford, Debbie Reynolds, and Rita Hayworth, with whom he starred in *Gilda*.

While I wasn't remotely tempted to have an affair with Glenn, from the first, he made it clear that he was eminently available to me. Although I didn't know it at the time, his attraction to me stemmed from a prediction by his psychic, the legendary Peter Hurkos, on whom Glenn was so dependent that he actually kept a spare bedroom in his house ready and waiting for Peter to stay in. During one of his psychic readings for Glenn, Peter had prophesied that Glenn and I were destined to be husband and wife. I did not concur. I made my lack of interest in Glenn obvious to him, but he still wasn't giving up. After all, he had the occult on his side.

New Year's Eve fell during the shooting of *The Courtship of Eddie's Father*, Glenn invited Jack and me to his New Year's Eve party at his home, near the Beverly Hills Hotel.

The evening was fun, and we all ate and drank a good deal, then toasted each other at midnight. A few moments into the New Year, Jack came over to me, somewhat sheepishly, and asked if I'd mind his visiting a friend's house round the corner, so he could have a quick New Year's drink with him. True to form, I didn't protest, although Jack's story was decidedly suspicious.

By two in the morning, there was no sign of Jack, and I was exhausted. In those days, mobile phones hadn't yet been invented. I didn't know where in hell Jack was, never mind with whom, so I just went upstairs and into the nearest bedroom, got straight into bed, and fell fast asleep, still wearing my ball gown.

I was out like a light until four in the morning, when I woke up with a start, to find Glenn Ford naked, except for his shorts, lying in bed next to me.

I jumped up and said, "I'm so sorry! Something terrible must have happened to Jack."

At that moment, the telephone rang.

Glenn answered. I couldn't hear Jack's end of the conversation, but I imagine he was apologizing profusely.

But Glenn was impervious. "You'd better get straight over here. Otherwise you won't have a wife anymore. . . ."

Within half an hour, Jack was banging on the front door. Glenn let him in and gave it to him straight: "How could you do this to your wife!"

Jack, always a quick thinker, came up with some excuse about an accident, they had been drinking, and on and on and on.

It was one of the few times in our marriage when I was so angry with Jack that I began to scream at him, yelling that I couldn't understand how he could treat me so badly.

Shocked by my confronting him, Jack apologized abjectly, then focused on his surroundings and realized that Glenn was dressed only in his shorts and that my ball gown was so crushed that it was obvious I'd been in bed.

I knew that even though Glenn and I had been in bed together, he hadn't tried anything sexual with me because I was soundly asleep, and I told Jack so. I don't know if Jack believed me or not or was actually jealous for the first time in our marriage, but if he was, he didn't show it. Instead, for the rest of his life, Jack always called Glenn Ford "the necrophiliac."

When all was said and done, though, Glenn Ford had behaved like a gentleman. So, in his Latin lover style, did Rossano Brazzi, who had starred in *South Pacific* and with whom I made a movie in Portugal in 1963. It was called *Dark Purpose* here and *L'intrigo* in Europe.

Sardonic actor George Sanders played my boss, an art dealer, I played a naïve American secretary, and Rossano played a mysterious count set on romancing me. As sometimes happens in movies, Rossano seemed fixated on continuing his role once the cameras had stopped rolling. When Rossano and I finished shooting our first scene, we ended up alone on the set together, and he started chasing me around the room.

When I backed away from him, he tried another approach: "Let's go out to dinner and then take a hotel room."

"What are you saying? I'm married! And so are you," was my instant reaction.

"We don't worry about that in Italy," retorted Rossano. "My wife doesn't mind what I do. I like what I do. She likes what I do. We could have a good time while we're on this movie. And Italian men don't go by the rules."

"Sorry, Rossano," I said firmly, "American women *do* go by the rules."

Marlon Brando, with whom I made *Bedtime Story* (which was later adapted into the musical *Dirty Rotten Scoundrels*), costarring David Niven, always lived his life by his own iconoclastic rules and ignored everyone else's.

The movie was partly filmed on location in Cannes, and in Hollywood. Marlon played Freddy Benson, a con man who dons a GI uniform to trick unsuspecting girls into bed, and David played Lawrence Jameson, the king of Riviera con men whose realm is threatened by the arrival of Freddy, and I played Janet Walker, the unwitting object of a bet between Freddy and Lawrence.

Before making *Bedtime Story*, Brando had

become disillusioned with making movies. The experience of filming *Mutiny on the Bounty* in Tahiti had soured him on working in movies. According to him, *Mutiny on the Bounty* had taken forever to make, and he had hated the director and conducted romantic affairs with practically every woman on the island of Tahiti.

Fortunately, he was happy to be making *Bedtime Story* because he had always wanted to do comedy, but no one in Hollywood had been prepared to give him that opportunity. So this uproarious comedy was his first shot, and he was thrilled. He also loved that he would be working with David Niven, whom he respected a great deal.

At the end of the first day of shooting, Brando asked me to come to his dressing room and talk. When I got there, ready to field the inevitable pass, I took a deep breath and said, "Marlon, I'm thrilled to be working with you and David. This is going to be fun for all of us."

"Yeah," Marlon mumbled, "I've had it with all the other crap." We chatted about the movie some more, and that was that. When we started working on our scenes together, it wasn't easy to work with him, particularly because director Ralph Levy was completely under his sway and allowed him free rein, so it was almost as if Brando himself were directing *Bedtime Story*.

Like Sinatra, Marlon was self-involved: everything he had to say or do was more important than anything anyone else had to say or do. However, unlike Sinatra, who was known in the business as "one-take Frank," Brando was never happy with the first, second, or third take. Part of the reason, I discovered, was because he was unable to remember any of his lines and had all of them written on the palms of his hands or on the side of a table.

Apart from that, he never got any scene right on the first take. Our first scene was straight-forward: we meet and he is desperately trying to seduce me. Nevertheless, it took sixty takes before Brando yelled cut. After that I understood why everyone always said Brando was America's greatest actor: he exhausted every other actor working with him!

He was never my favorite actor, either on-screen or off. Despite his image as the ultimate sex symbol, I wasn't in the least bit turned on by kissing Brando during the scene when I rub oil all over him on the beach. While he was a great kisser, he was not the best I've ever had. (That distinction goes first to Burt Lancaster, and then to Richard Widmark.) But apart from that, shooting love scenes is never sexually exciting. You are too busy remembering what you are doing, your lines, the next bit of dialogue . . .

Brando really wanted to make a success of *Bedtime Story* because he had always longed to play comedy, and this was his chance. He had great respect for David Niven and his work, and he didn't make David do so many takes. At the end of shooting each day, Marlon and I would sit around while David told great stories, and Marlon was fascinated.

When the picture wrapped, David invited Marlon, Jack and me, and a group of David's friends to dinner at his house in Brentwood.

When we arrived on the porch, Marlon's best friend, Wally Cox, who had started out in New York with Brando at the beginning of his career and always made him laugh, with Cox's quirky sense of humor, rushed up to us and said, "Marlon is here, but he doesn't want to face his son. So don't be surprised by what you see when you come into the house."

Jack and I walked into the living room, where a huge table was filled with all kinds of food. Underneath the table was Marlon, sitting cross-legged, hiding from his son.

He stayed that way for a couple of hours, then, without a word, got up and rushed out into the night. Some bedtime story. . . .

In *Elmer Gantry*, I had a seminude scene, but I was to venture further into nudity in the TV movie *Silent Night, Lonely Night*, which I made in 1969. It was based on Robert Anderson's play of the same name, which had been produced on Broadway with Henry Fonda and Barbara Bel Geddes.

Silent Night, Lonely Night movingly told the story of a couple who, by chance, meet on Christmas Eve, when they are both riding on a bus to Amherst. She is visiting her son in school there, though her heart is heavy as she is aware that her husband is having an affair. The man is visiting his wife in a mental hospital and knows that when he arrives, she will no longer recognize him.

Along the way, he recounts the story of his first affair to the woman, an affair with the town groupie, with whom he had sex one night in the empty school gym. As he relates what happened, my character fantasizes about being the town groupie and having sex with him.

Before we shot that scene, Danny Petrie, *Silent Night, Lonely Night*'s director, gingerly approached me and asked how I would feel about taking my clothes off. I was torn between agreeing and refusing because, after all, this was a TV movie and who knew whether a nude scene would get past the strict censors.

Danny reassured me that *Silent Night, Lonely Night* was slated for a theatrical release, and that I'd only be seen topless and from behind.

He promised, too, that he would clear the set, which he did when we eventually shot the scene. During my nude scene, Lloyd Bridges, my costar, was kind and understanding and helped me not to feel too self-conscious. Thanks to him, the scene went well, and when *Silent Night, Lonely Night* was released, I was thrilled to be nominated for my first Emmy.

I did my second nude scene with Lloyd as well, when we made *The Happy Ending* together in 1969. I played Flo, a good-time girl who's had a series of affairs with married men; our costar was Bobby Darin, who played the hustler Franco.

Bobby always seemed to me to be an extremely tortured man, despite his charm and great talent. As we grew closer and closer as friends, he gave me the great compliment of confiding his biggest secret to me. I became the first person to whom he revealed his shattering discovery that the woman who he had thought was his sister was in reality his mother. "That has ruined my life," he said. "All my life, everyone has lied to me. To grow up believing that the woman you thought was your mother was actually your grandmother, and your sister was really your mother, and then only finding out the news when you were an adult, is devastating."

Much later, he was diagnosed with a form of blood poisoning and was angry that he was going to die. "I hate everybody I am leaving behind," he said to me.

By the time I made *The Happy Ending* I wasn't in the least bit inhibited anymore about doing a nude scene, nor was Jack in the least bit jealous that I did it. In fact, he was actually turned on by my appearing on-screen in the nude.

Soon, though, I would give him something tangible about which to be jealous—my very first, and extremely adulterous, love affair with another man.

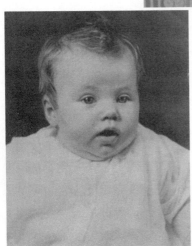

"Looking at the world with wonder." August 8, 1934.

I told my mother I hated bows.

Singing in the choir at twelve.

Happy in my late teens.

Me in high school.

With my proud parents after winning Miss Pittsburgh 1952.

At the prom with
Bill Boninni.

With my
former beau
Lou Malone.

In *April Love* and even more in love with Jack than ever.

Mae West and me in her fur wrap during the heat wave.

Gordon sings "The Surrey with the Fringe on Top." He had the most glorious voice ever.

"Oh, What a Beautiful Morning" (from *Oklahoma!*).

The death
scene in
Carousel.
(My first
crying
scene.)

Me and my mentor
Burt Lancaster in
Elmer Gantry.

Winning the Academy Award for my part as Lulu Baines in *Elmer Gantry*.

As Marian the librarian.

As Marian
the librarian
and extremely
pregnant in
*The Music
Man*.

James Cagney
and me in an
*un*romantic
scene from
*Never Steal
Anything
Small*.

Marlon Brando on the beach in *Bedtime Story*.

With Jimmy Stewart in one of my favorite
scenes from one of my favorite movies,
The Cheyenne Social Club.

I live out one of Jack's fantasies by dressing up as a Playboy Bunny.

On a TV show with Glenn Ford before I inadvertently slept in his bed.

Jack and me at a Hollywood costume party.

A happy family with Jack, Shaun, and baby Patrick.

Me and Shaun.

Jack, me, Shaun, and Patrick.

A classic moment of closeness between David and me during *The Partridge Family*.

Jack and me during our fateful Las Vegas show. Jack is showing the strain.

The Partridge Family in
their heyday.

December 18,
1974. Marty and
me on our first
date and the
very first time
of many when
he made me
laugh.

Wedding day with Marty, 1977.

Marty and me on our first Christmas together. I am surrounded by all the gifts Marty gave me.

The lines are drawn on Patrick's wedding day.

I get my star on Hollywood Boulevard. (The one next to John Wayne's!)

Eat your heart out,
Florence
Henderson!

With President
Reagan and
First Lady
Nancy Reagan.

174

At the White House with President George Bush and First Lady Barbara Bush.

In my Emmy Award–nominated performance in *Hidden Places* in 2006. As Aunt Batty, with aging makeup to complete the look.

A rare quiet moment.

True love—Marty and me.

EIGHT

Out of My Dreams

By 1965, Hollywood studios were no longer making many blockbuster musicals, and worse still, I wasn't getting the kind of roles I'd hoped for after I won the Academy Award for *Elmer Gantry*.

So I took a deep breath, braced myself, and signed to headline in my own all-singing, all-dancing cabaret show at the Flamingo Hotel, Las Vegas.

The show was due to open in April 1965. In those days, Las Vegas shows ran for five or six weeks, so when I attended my first rehearsal, I knew I was there for the long haul, and I was on my own, as Jack was in Manhattan, starring on Broadway with Carol Burnett in *Fade Out—Fade In*.

My show was a potpourri of my singing songs from all my movies and dancing in a copy of the sexy slip I wore in *Elmer Gantry*. I enjoyed rehearsing for my act and looked forward to opening night.

My sons were with me in Las Vegas, along with

the nanny, and apart from missing Jack, only one other factor disturbed me: as I danced and sang my way through rehearsals at the Flamingo Hotel every single day, a bald, not particularly attractive, older man sat in the front row and watched me like a hawk.

On my last day of rehearsals, Hal Belfer, the entertainment manager of the Flamingo, sidled up to me and said, "Shirley, that gentleman who always sits in the front row watching your rehearsal is madly smitten with you. He is a very special guest of the Flamingo and owns five oil wells, so I'd appreciate it if after your opening night, you would go and have a drink with him, then go gambling with him."

I was shocked, but not surprised. Like everyone else who played Vegas during those years, I knew the score. The Mafia ruled Las Vegas with a rod of iron. (The Flamingo, of course, was once owned by Bugsy Siegel.) Socializing with wealthy gamblers after the show was expected of entertainers like me. Gordon MacRae's wife, Sheila, was told exactly the same thing by the bosses when she played Las Vegas, to gamble with special high rollers after her show. That's how things were in Las Vegas in those days. I knew better than not to cooperate with the all-powerful men who ran the town, so, much as I didn't want to, I agreed to gamble with the bald gentleman after my show.

Jack didn't come to my opening night, as he was still working on Broadway. But true to my agreement with the management, after I'd finished my first show, I had a drink with the bald gentleman.

He was pleasant enough and told me about his business, the oil wells he owned, and I told him about my two children, Shaun and Patrick, and about my husband, Jack Cassidy. Undeterred by my marital status, he asked me to gamble with him. Mindful of my agreement with Hal Belfer and the Flamingo Hotel, despite my better instincts, I accepted his invitation.

As we sat down at the tables, he handed me a wad of cash and insisted that I use it to gamble. I protested, but he wouldn't listen, so I gave in reluctantly. We placed our bets, and to my surprise, I won. So did he. And at the end of the evening, he handed me $500 and said, "It's yours."

The following night, the same bald man was in the front row of my show again. When it was over, as the audience applauded me, I was showered with green flowers. Then a messenger ran up to the stage with armfuls of gifts, all in various shades of green. All of this, I discovered later, was from the bald man, who had, in our conversation the previous night, discovered that green was my favorite color.

By that time, I had learned that bald man was Mike Davis. A larger-than-life character, he was the owner of Tiger Oil and really did own oil wells. No wonder Hal Belfer had asked me to gamble with him after the show. He was a high roller, and that meant big bucks to the Flamingo Hotel. I knew better than to flout the management by refusing to sit at the tables with Mr. Davis after my show every night.

So each night, when Mike and I had finished gambling, I went upstairs to my suite and there was another gift from him spread out on the bed: a mink coat, a diamond bracelet, emerald earrings. I returned every gift to him as politely as possible, but he refused to give up and the gifts from him kept on coming.

My show ran over the Easter weekend, and Shaun and Patrick, their nanny, and I were sitting round the hotel pool, having fun, when Mike Davis suddenly materialized, carrying a vast basket of hand-blown Easter eggs. The boys were thrilled with his gift, even more so when they discovered that inside each egg was a $100 bill.

I was touched and thanked Mike profusely, but as more gifts arrived for me, I carried on turning them down as graciously as possible. But he kept pressuring me to let him buy me something, anything, just so that I had something from him.

In the end, I capitulated to the full force of his will and allowed him to buy me a hand-cut emerald ring and another ring with a precious green stone (but not an emerald). I accepted Mike's gifts as politely as was possible.

To my relief, he never once made a pass at me.

Finally, at the very end of the run of my Las Vegas show, Jack flew into town and came to see the show at last. Afterward, he and I and a bunch of our friends had cocktails together in the hotel lounge. Meanwhile, Mike Davis was at his usual table across the room, gambling with hundreds of thousands of dollars. Now and again, he caught my eye. I looked away, but I knew patently well that he wanted me to come over and gamble with him as I always did. But I was with Jack and our friends, so I studiously ignored Mike.

Finally, Hal Belfer came over to our table and said, "Mr. Davis would like you to come over to his table and do a little gambling with him."

It was time for me to make a stand. I drew myself up to my full height and said, "Hal, this is my husband, Jack Cassidy. Please give Mr. Davis my apologies and tell him that I can't gamble with him tonight as my husband is here with me."

Hal went over to Mike Davis and broke the news to him. Whereupon Mike stood up, ripped a $100 bill into pieces, and made for the exit. As he did, he kept ripping up $100 bills and throwing the pieces all over the casino floor. Security came over and warned him he was going to cause a riot, but Mike didn't care.

"I can do what I want," he said, and threw

another wad of ripped-up $100 bills onto the floor, while crowds of onlookers dived to pick up the pieces, pocket them, and stick them together again afterward.

The very next day, I discovered that I was pregnant (with my son Ryan, after Jack and I had had a romantic night during my Vegas run), then I had to leave for Lake Tahoe where I was doing my last engagement of the tour. A few days later, Mike Davis called me up there, and I flatly informed him that our relationship—such as it was—was over.

He was devastated and said, "Listen, if you agree to see me again, I'll give you an oil well."

"No, Mike, I can't see you again. I'm going to have a baby, Tahoe is my last gig, and I'm married to Jack."

After a moment's silence, Mike finally said, "Don't you know your husband is fucking every woman in Manhattan?" Mike couldn't wait to tell me every detail of Jack's manifold infidelities.

"I don't want to hear that," I said.

"Well, I don't know why you are being so true to him when he is fucking everyone in town."

"That's my business, not yours." I hung up on Mike.

When I told Jack what had happened, he just laughed. "Take the oil well, Mouse. And if he really wants to see you, I'll come with you."

Jack's pragmatic advice aside, I never saw Mike Davis again.

However, after Jack died, Mike called me up and offered to fly anyone I wanted to Los Angeles for the funeral. He also offered to pay for all the funeral expenses. I thanked him, but turned him down as politely as I could and told him that the funeral was not going to be big. Soon after that, Phyllis McGuire, the youngest of the McGuire Sisters, who gained notoriety through her relationship with mobster Sam Giancana, became Mike Davis's long-term companion.

After I finished playing Tahoe, Ryan, our third son, was born. I was delighted, and so was Jack, although sometimes the stress of having three little boys under one roof became too much for him. Brought up by his strict mother to be fastidious in the extreme, Jack imposed his own rigid standards on the boys. They weren't allowed to make a single noise all morning when he was sleeping the day away after a drunken binge.

He wanted everything to be neat and always in its own place, but that was a tall order for three normal, rambunctious little boys. Jack's high standards were impossible to maintain, and if he came home to find a toy or two scattered on the floor, he invariably erupted in anger. As he screamed at our hapless little boys, who were shaking from head to foot out of fear of their father, I couldn't help wondering if he was screaming at them or at the universe for not granting him the movie career he craved.

Meanwhile, I wasn't having much of a movie career anymore myself. Instead, in the winter of 1966, I signed to do a tour of *The Sound of Music* and took my sons with me, along with their nanny. As always, Jack was appearing on Broadway, this time in *It's a Bird . . . It's a Plane . . . It's Superman*, with Linda Lavin and Patricia Marand, and this time the rumors that he was having an affair with an actress in the show were deafening. I was led to understand by "well-wishers" that this was not Jack's usual type of lighthearted sexual fling but a full-blown love affair, and that the woman was doing everything in her power to incite him to divorce me and marry her.

Whatever the truth, I intended to remain married to Jack, no matter what or whom. There had always been other women in Jack's life, I knew, but this time was different. He was pulling away from me emotionally, and I could sense it in the very fibers of my being. And to top that, I also had the feeling that he was disappointed that I hadn't had an affair with Mike Davis. In a strange, perverse way, Jack actually wanted me to be unfaithful to him.

The Sound of Music, which began in January 1967, took me to theaters all over the East Coast, and we usually traveled from venue to venue by car. Inevitably, my costar Stephen Elliott (who would go on to play Liza Minnelli's father in

Arthur) was by my side. At forty-seven, he was a complete gentleman, erudite, well read, charming, Captain Von Trapp to my Maria.

I suppose what happened next was inevitable.

It all began with a party in Stephen's room after the show's opening night. My own three kids, who were traveling with me, were fast asleep in my room, watched over by their nanny.

Gradually, all the guests left, and suddenly Steve and I were alone together. Then he grabbed me and kissed me, really kissed me. Despite myself, despite my marriage, despite my love for my husband, I had to admit that Steve's kisses felt more than good. When he led me to the bed, things went further; I acquiesced.

For the first time in my marriage, I was unfaithful to Jack. And I didn't feel guilty at all. At last, the goose was doing the same thing as the gander. . . .

Against my better judgment and all my principles, I enjoyed my affair with Stephen Elliott. He was bright, intellectual, and had a great sense of humor. We talked a great deal, and I learned a lot from him. Unlike Jack—who was all about Jack —Stephen was riveted by me and wanted to know everything about me. He studied me intently, my character, my desires, my likes, and dislikes.

Unlike Jack, Stephen was 100 percent interested in me. In how I looked, what I wore, what I said, where I went, how I handled my kids. Whereas Jack was only interested in Jack.

Within a few days, Stephen knew me better than Jack ever had, even down to observing, "You are beautiful everywhere, except your feet." I felt loved, wanted, and he made me laugh (my fatal weakness).

Toward the end of the tour, Jack came up to visit me and to see the show. Afterward, we had dinner with Stephen, and he and Jack appeared to get on really well, and I was relieved.

However, back in our room, when I was already in bed and Jack was getting undressed, he suddenly turned round and said, "So how is your affair with Stephen going?"

"What did you say?" I said, playing dumb.

"You are having an affair with him, aren't you?"

I had no intention of confessing the truth. What had happened between Stephen and me belonged to us, not Jack. It was our private story and I wanted it to stay that way.

So I looked Jack straight in the eyes and said, "No, Jack. Why, in heaven's name, are you saying that?"

"Come on, Shirl, it was really obvious to me tonight."

"Jack," I said firmly, "Stephen and I are good friends, and that's it."

Jack smiled. "Sure you are . . . but it's okay."

He knew—he just knew!—and he was almost thrilled. Later on, he interrogated me about what happened between Stephen and me in bed and made it obvious that he wanted to know all the details of my sex life with Stephen. Moreover, the thought of my having an affair with another man had clearly made Jack even hotter for me.

But I still kept denying that I had had an affair with Stephen Elliott. It belonged to me, not Jack, and that was how I intended it to stay. You could say that I conducted my extramarital affair with Stephen in exactly the same way as Jack had conducted his extramarital affairs with all of his women: no guilt, no confessions, and no repercussions. I guess I learned to do that just by watching Jack and following his example.

In the end, Stephen ended it between us. "You are still very much in love with your husband, and that's obvious," he said.

I admitted that he was right, and I was. I loved Jack as much as ever, but I had had fun with Stephen. Everyone in the show probably knew the truth. Stephen was single, and afterward he said that what happened between us had been wonderful. And in the true show-business tradition of "On location, nothing counts," when the show ended, so did our affair.

It was a charming interlude, but my heart was never in it.

Despite Jack's nonchalance regarding my affair with Stephen, he still wanted to remain married to me. To that end, he suggested that we work together again, which was financially beneficial to us, but also meant that I would be transported back to the early days of our love affair, when we worked together on the European tour of *Oklahoma!* and Jack was my costar and my mentor.

So Jack came up with the idea of our doing a tour of *Wait Until Dark*, in which I would play the part of the blind girl, Susy Hendrix, and he would play the villain, Harry Roat Jr. Jack had had plenty of experience in playing villains during his career (from Macheath in *The Threepenny Opera* to the murderer Leonard Vole in Agatha Christie's *Witness for the Prosecution*), but I had never played a blind girl before.

I spent three weeks at The Lighthouse, a New York center for the blind, where I studied blind people. I learned that no two blind people handle their disability in the same way, and that a blind woman is more likely to veer to the left, and a blind man is more likely to veer to the right. I also consulted with Lee Remick, who created the part of Susy Hendrix in the original Broadway production of *Wait Until Dark*.

I prepared for the part of Susy by learning to keep my eyes out of focus, a difficult thing to do, but crucial when playing someone blind.

Jack was brilliant as Roat, and during one particularly harrowing scene, he had to hit me hard, something neither of us relished. But the scene was crucial to the plot, so we both went along with it.

Before the tour began, we held a full dress rehearsal for our family and friends. Ryan, who was then just two years old, was in the audience, in retrospect, an unwise decision on our part. When we got to the scene in which Jack went for it and started to hit me, Ryan began screaming pitifully, "Look, Daddy's hitting Mommy! Daddy's hitting Mommy!"

The entire audience turned and stared at him in horror. Jack and I froze for a second, then fled from the stage into the auditorium, where Ryan was crying his heart out. We both held him, comforted him, and assured him, "Don't be upset, baby, it's only a play."

After that, we made sure that our sons never saw either of us in any of our performances that might upset them. And I banned them from seeing me in *Elmer Gantry* until they were way into their teens.

During the run of *Wait Until Dark* I found that working with Jack was wonderful, as always. I learned so much from him when we were onstage together—how to move better, how to project more. His stage presence was magical, and some of it always rubbed off on me.

So I was thrilled when my manager, Ruth Aarons, called with the news that Jack and I had been offered the leading roles in a Broadway musical to be called *Maggie Flynn*. We both read the script, listened to the music, and adored it. Besides, we loved the idea of continuing to work together, and not being separated on two different coasts.

The show and the parts were wonderful for both of us, and I luxuriated in the joy of having Jack sing romantic ballads to me onstage once more, just as he had in *Oklahoma!* at the start of our love affair.

In *Maggie Flynn*, I played an Irish lady living in the Bronx during the Civil War, a time in which the authorities were kidnapping black children and taking them away from New York. My character, Maggie Flynn, decided that she wanted to protect them and keep them safe in her basement apartment.

Jack played Phineas Finn, my husband, a circus clown, who, in a twist of the plot slightly reminiscent of my offstage life with Jack, had disappeared. Consequently, I had a boyfriend, Colonel John Farraday, who wanted me to divorce my errant husband and marry him instead. So John and I became secretly engaged.

Then Phineas suddenly arrives back on the scene again, and I fall for him once more. Jack was playing himself, a philanderer who was no good and who ended up in jail. But in *Maggie Flynn*, as in real life, I still loved him.

Away from the theater, Jack and I rented that castle in Irvington-on-Hudson, and all the kids—including David—lived up there with us.

The show, which opened on October 23, 1968, was beautiful, in particular the ending, when Jack walks on the stage from one wing, and I from the other, and we meet in the middle and sing a duet together, "Mr. Clown." The audience always went crazy for this moving, emotional song and seemed to love the show as a whole.

However, for some unknown reason that, to this day, I am unable to fathom, after just three and a half months the producers closed the show. We had no notice. It was a fait accompli.

I was deeply disappointed, but Jack took the closure far harder than I did. He had great hopes that he would win a Tony for *Maggie Flynn*. After all, he had already won one for his acclaimed performance in *She Loves Me* and had also been nominated for *Superman*, and *Fade Out—Fade In*, and I thought he should have won for both. So he had every reason to believe that he could win a Tony for his performance in *Maggie Flynn*, and that I could win one as well. Jack was indeed nominated for a Best Actor Tony for his part as Phineas, but was beaten by Jerry Orbach in *Promises, Promises*. And even if Jack had won, he would still have been devastated that the show closed so early in the run. As always, he drowned his sorrows in drink.

Drink as he did, at that stage in his life Jack was still far too much in control to let his drinking end up damaging his career. To Jack, drinking didn't just revolve around the lure of the alcohol but around the camaraderie of hanging out with other guys and shooting the breeze together until the early hours of the morning. That was what really mattered to him.

One evening, after the curtain fell on whichever Broadway show Jack was then starring in, he ended up hanging out at the Copa, as he often did. That particular evening, Johnny Carson was drinking alone at the bar, so Jack joined him, and they had a couple of drinks together. Then Jack moved on to another table to join a couple of friends.

After a while, the bartender came over and said, "Jack, you've gotta help me out. Johnny is as drunk as a skunk, and I'm afraid he's gonna hurt himself, or somebody else. We've got to get him out of here."

So Jack went over and said, "Come on, Johnny, I'll take you wherever you want to go, and we'll have a drink on the way."

Johnny fought him and refused to quit drinking, but in the end Jack got him to leave and got him home in once piece.

Many times after that night, Jack did Johnny's show, but Johnny never mentioned that Jack had rescued him from a drunken binge at the Copa.

Johnny was a difficult, enigmatic man, but when he died, he secretly left a vast fortune to a variety of children's foundations and women's organizations, all under an assumed name.

Generally, Jack aroused positive feelings in both men and women. Once, though, he was invited to attend Burt Reynolds's roast and came out with a funny line about Burt. Burt lashed back with "While you're up here, Marty Ingels is walking around in your bathrobe and slippers." Jack knew Burt quite well and just laughed his comments off.

Jack was a great raconteur and an amusing drinking buddy. George C. Scott was another of Jack's drinking comrades and a close friend. George produced *The Andersonville Trial*, in which Jack appeared in 1970 and for which he got an Emmy nomination.

However, close as Jack and George were, both Jack and I knew that George was a split personality: a delight when he was drinking, but a monster when he was drunk. One night when he was dating a young actress, Jack and I had a lovely dinner with the two of them at our home, and then they hung out with us in the backyard afterward. George and Jack started drinking pretty heavily, but as I had to get up and go to work extremely early the next morning, I made my excuses and went up to bed. Soon after, his girlfriend also went up to bed and left George and Jack alone together, still drinking.

I was just dropping off to sleep when I heard an almighty crash, which was clearly the sound of a bottle being smashed to smithereens. I ran downstairs, and there was George, holding a broken bottle up against Jack's cheek, yelling, "Unless you tell me the truth, I'm going to stab you to death."

Jack, never one to lose his cool, even under the direst circumstances, started to edge away from George, extremely gingerly, saying, "You don't have to do this, George, we're friends."

Luckily, at that moment, George saw me standing on the threshold. I gave him a stern look, whereupon he dropped the bottle and said, "I gotta go."

I never did discover why he was threatening Jack, and what he wanted Jack to tell him.

After *Maggie Flynn* closed, I was cast in *The Cheyenne Social Club*, which Gene Kelly directed and was to be shot in Santa Fe, New Mexico. I played Jenny, the madam of a brothel, the Cheyenne Social Club. The script was a delight, my role was fun, and I was glad that Jimmy Stewart and Henry Fonda were to be my costars.

As this was my second movie with Jimmy (the first was *Two Rode Together*), I was extremely comfortable working with him. Moreover, he was such a natural and always ready to help his fellow actors.

Working with Henry Fonda, however, wasn't as

much of a picnic. He was so remote, so cold, so unlike Jimmy, that it was hard for me to believe that they were best friends.

Henry Fonda made it extremely clear from the start that he didn't want to communicate with me or anyone else on the movie, other than Jimmy.

Whenever we met in makeup, Fonda would be sitting in the makeup chair, ramrod straight, and I would say, "Hi, Hank, how are you?"

He would just look away and make sure that there was no eye contact between us. I never got to know who he was as a human being, which was probably his intention and just the way he liked it.

I didn't let Fonda's remoteness trouble me. I was so happy working with Jimmy, and I loved my part and the script and everything else connected with the movie.

Besides, I had just read the best TV-pilot script I'd ever read—for a show to be called *The Partridge Family*.

NINE

The Partridge Family

By now, David Cassidy, my stepson, was in his late teens. Through the years, I'd felt sorry for him when Jack was too hard on him, particularly when my kids, Shaun, Patrick, and Ryan, were born, and I felt Jack didn't give David nearly enough attention. But I soon revised my opinion because, as time went on, Jack didn't give our kids together that much attention, either.

In his early teens, David let his hair grow long, until it reached right down to his shoulders, and Jack wasn't crazy about that, nor, it transpired, was my mother. When I was pregnant with Ryan and had just a week to go before my cesarean was scheduled, she came to stay so that she could help me when the baby was born. Fifteen-year-old David was staying with us. My mother took one look at David, with his shoulder-length hair, and said, "David, that hair looks terrible!"

David declared defiantly, "I like it!"

Undeterred, my mother, who, I realized in retrospect, was blind drunk, ran out of the room, got a pair of scissors, and tried to cut David's hair.

David dodged my mother as best he could and yelled, "Get away from me!"

Horrified, I jumped in and grabbed the scissors from my mother. David breathed a sigh of relief, and peace within the family was restored, among the kids at least. But not for me. Twenty minutes later, I went into labor from sheer shock at what my mother had almost done to poor David, and soon afterward, on February 23, 1966, Ryan was born!

In his teens, David continued on his path as an inveterate womanizer. My son Patrick, too, turned out to be very sexually oriented. Just like his father, and, to be honest, just like me, as well.

When Patrick was thirteen, I was cooking pancakes one morning when he came running down the stairs shouting, "Mom, Mom!"

"What happened, honey?"

"Mom, I've just had my first orgasm. I woke up, and it happened!"

"What?!"

"Does it often happen when you wake up?"

I nodded, not exactly sure what to say next, and I certainly did not want to raise the subject with Jack, who could be a strict and autocratic father, as David sadly learned many times in his young life.

When David was starting out in the theater, and auditioning for jobs, plus attending acting classes whenever he could, Jack insisted that David take a part-time job and found him one himself.

Jack meant well for his eldest son, I know, trying to instill self-reliance and independence in him, but Jack still made an error of judgment when he got David a thankless job starting out in the mail room of a textile company based in New York City. David was paid $2 an hour, which netted him $38 a week, which hardly paid for his train fare commuting from Irvington-on-Hudson into the city each day.

Jack also suddenly decreed that David should not wear his habitual uniform of a trusty pair of jeans, a T-shirt, and tennis shoes to work every day.

One Saturday, in classic-Jack grand-seigneur style, he announced to David that he was taking him into the city to buy him a suit. David was overwhelmed by Jack's sudden burst of fatherly interest and generosity and was ecstatic.

So Jack took David to Jack's very own tailor, Roland Meledandri, and first selected two suits for himself. Then he turned his attention to David and selected not only a suit for him, but also a stylish overcoat, a flawless sports jacket, and a perfect pair of slacks. David was overjoyed, even more so when the bill for those clothes was presented: $800! His father had spent $800 on him!

Poor David came down with an unpleasant bump,

however, when Jack informed him that David now owed him $800. Every single solitary cent of it. And that Jack expected David to start paying it off at $15 a week. Almost half his $38 weekly salary. To his credit, David worked like a dog and ultimately paid Jack back every single cent.

Yet, David felt that his father had tricked him into going into debt and felt betrayed. I couldn't blame David one iota.

But to do Jack justice, he did try to help David launch his show-business career. Jack paid a photographer to shoot professional photographs of David, then found him an agent and, most important of all, prevailed on our manager, Ruth Aarons, to manage David as well.

I was glad that his professional life was taking positive shape so early on. Through the years, even when he was a small child, David was always on my side, was never cheeky to me or disobedient. I think he respected me, and whatever I said, went. On the other hand, while he was always nice to me, good to me, we never sat down and had long talks, and he never sent me birthday cards or Christmas presents, unless he was staying with us. We only really got to know each other properly when we made *The Partridge Family* together.

Right before I was cast in *The Partridge Family*, I remember coming out of the house late one afternoon and finding David, who was baby-sitting that night, in the pool playing with Shaun.

I was wearing a micro-miniskirt and a tight sweater as I was on my way to have dinner with an agent.

Shaun looked me up and down. "Why do you dress that way, Mom? No other mother dresses that way. It's because you are going to do that show. . . ."

Outraged, and extremely protective of me as always, David rounded on Shaun. "What do you mean! You've got a beautiful mother, and why shouldn't she show her legs?"

Shaun clammed up, and that was that.

Before I was offered the part of Shirley Partridge in *The Partridge Family*, I was offered the leading role of Carol Ann Martin, the mother in *The Brady Bunch*, the role later played by Florence Henderson. Now that my kids were old enough to be attending school and couldn't take time off to come on location with me, I was eager to work in TV, so that I wouldn't have to be away making movies and not see my kids for weeks on end. While the idea of playing the mother in *The Brady Bunch* was initially attractive to me, I turned it down because I didn't want to be the mother taking the roast out of the oven and not doing much else. Besides, my agent and my manager were both adamant that taking part in a TV series would inevitably lead to the death of my career as a movie star.

I didn't really care if they were right. Spending time with my kids mattered more to me than anything else, and if giving up movies and appearing in a TV show instead would facilitate that, I was happy.

So when my agent came to me with an offer to do the pilot for a TV series called *The Partridge Family*, I studied the script extremely carefully and quickly realized from the get-go that it was very different from the saga of the mom taking the roast out of the oven. Shirley Partridge was a working mother, *The Partridge Family* was a family who actually worked together, stayed together, laughed together, and liked one another in the bargain.

The show was born during the post-Monkees era when, one night, writer Bernard Slade, who created *The Flying Nun* and later the hit play *Same Time, Next Year*, was watching the Johnny Carson show and the Cowsills came on. This family-turned-pop-group was formed in 1965 by Barbara, the mother; and her kids, Bob, Barry, Bill, John, Susan, and Paul. In 1967 and 1968, the Cowsills had hits with "Indian Lake," "The Rain, the Park & Other Things," and "Poor Baby."

The show *The Sound of Music* was big right then, so Bernard Slade came up with the idea of creating a sitcom about a traveling family pop group. Initially his concept was to have the Cowsills play themselves, but then he met with them and discovered that none of them had any acting experience, and, worse still, only one family member had much personality. So Bernard decided to hire actors instead.

The show, conceived as a middle-of-the-road situation comedy with music, was initially going to be called *The Family Business*. However, Bernard had gone to school in England and had played soccer there. The center-half was a boy named Partridge. Hence his inspiration for the name Partridge.

The Partridge Family was a little different from most other shows on television at that time, and the plan was that we would sing a new song each show.

More important than my like of the artistic concept of the show were the private benefits for me. I had no doubts at all about playing Shirley Partridge. First, because she was destined to become the first working mother on TV and I loved the script. Second, because working on the series would let me be an almost full-time mom and raise my kids. I had always relished being a mom, and I would probably have had eight kids if I could. Above all, I wanted to be a different kind of mom from my own mom. And I was sure that I didn't want to miss my kids' growing up because I was always away on location without them because they were now back home and at school.

So without my having to attend a single

audition, I was offered the role of Shirley Partridge in *The Partridge Family* and was hired on the spot. Jack, however, was not in the least bit enthralled by the prospect of my becoming Shirley Partridge. He thought *The Partridge Family* was trivial and didn't mince words in giving me his opinion. His opinion, however, was not based purely on his artistic judgment. In truth, Jack, like most actors, wanted to be the star of a TV show himself. The last thing that he wanted was for his wife to become a TV star when he wasn't.

Not to mention his eldest son . . .

David, who was aiming to become a serious actor and had so far appeared on a number of hit TV shows such as *Bonanza*, didn't want to test for *The Partridge Family*. He, too, considered it lightweight. But his manager, and mine, Ruth Aarons, convinced him to go for it. So without Jack's or my knowing it, he went over to Screen Gems and read for Renée Valente, the casting director, and Paul Junger Witt, the producer/director, and auditioned for the part of Keith Partridge.

The casting director and the producers liked David enough to invite him back for a screen test, but they wondered how I would feel about working with my stepson. They were afraid that my off-set relationship with him might cause problems between us on set. So they asked me what I thought about working with David on the show.

I said I had no problems working with him whatsoever. "David is my stepson, not my son. I didn't raise him and I won't be tempted to baby him. He's a good actor, a good singer, and we have a great relationship."

With that obstacle removed, the producers breathed a big sigh of relief and screen-tested David, even though at nineteen he was probably far too old to play Keith Partridge, a high school kid. Fortunately for him, he was small for his age, and much as he would come to hate it, he could still pass for a high school kid. So David was cast to play Keith for a weekly salary of $600.

On the first day of rehearsals, I already knew that David was in the cast, but he had no idea that I was, as well. So when I walked on set, he was completely surprised and asked what I was doing there.

"I'm playing your mama in this, sweetheart."

For once, David was lost for words. Fortunately for both of us, and for the series, our first scene together turned out to be wonderful. As we worked together in the series, David became more and more aware of me. He would come up to me after we'd finished for the day and say things like "Wow! How do you do it? You are so good in every scene." He began to respect me as an actress, and our relationship blossomed on a professional as well as a personal level.

Jack, however, was extremely jealous that David was in *The Partridge Family* with me. To be fair to Jack, he said from the start that he thought David was taking a wrong career path, that he'd be far better off taking singing and acting lessons and working on Broadway instead.

I didn't necessarily agree with Jack, but as a stepmother, I always tried to remain outside of the arguments between Jack and David.

The pilot of *The Partridge Family* was filmed in Los Angeles and Las Vegas. I played a widow who hears her children sing in the garage, where they have formed a band, and they convince her to join, although she can't sing a single note. The precocious young genius, Danny (played by Danny Bonaduce), the middle child of the family, slips a recording of them singing under the toilet stall occupied by agent Reuben Kincaid, played by Dave Madden, a rubber-faced comedy star who had appeared in *Camp Runamuck* and *Rowan & Martin's Laugh-In*.

Kincaid (who was to become the comic foil to Danny Bonaduce's character) plays the disc and is impressed by what he hears and decides to represent the Partridge Family. By some miracle, he books them to play Las Vegas, and they travel there on a bus that they have painted in garish colors. They make their debut at Caesars Palace, Las Vegas, and are an overnight sensation.

From then on, the original intention of the series was that it would follow the Partridge Family's adventures in show business. That changed down the line to more of a focus on the domestic and private life of the family—whose members didn't resemble each other in the least! The fans neither noticed nor cared.

I had top billing in the show, which aired on Friday nights at 8:30 p.m. The initial plan had been that I would be the band's lead singer on the show, but then Ruth Aarons suggested David for the part of Keith Partridge and informed the producers that he could sing and play instruments, as well, and would be terrific singing all the songs, which were happy-go-lucky, light, and positive. Once the producers heard David sing and play, they decided that he was perfect and would make a wonderful lead singer for the band. I was happy for him.

I had a strong sense that the show would be a hit. It was new and funny and the music was good, and David had a chance to make it as a teen idol. The music wasn't my thing, but I felt that it could succeed with the kids of this new generation.

The Partridge Family pilot was shot on the Columbia Ranch, now the Warner Ranch, on Sound Stage 30, with the entire Partridge home constructed on the set. After the first episode aired on September 25, 1970, the reviewers were anything but ecstatic. The *Christian Science Monitor* sniped, "The show stacks implausibility upon implausibility from the hit record to the psychedelic bus they tool around in."

Audiences, however, liked the show from the first. We, the cast, were all elated about the audience response to our show. In particular, David loved appearing on *The Partridge Family*. The months before he became a rock-star sensation were the best time of his life. Suddenly he was acting, he was in the company of people whom he respected. He did all the jokes in the show, he got all the laughs, and for the first time in his life he was winning the respect of his peers, and he loved it.

When we all started working together on *The Partridge Family*, we were a happy family, although nine-year-old Jeremy Gelbwaks, who played Chris Partridge, turned out to be a handful. He would zoom around the studio making the sound of a jet plane and crash into people.

Jeremy lasted one season as Chris Partridge. He was replaced in the show by eleven-year-old Brian Forster, whose step-grandfather, Alan Napier, played the butler in the TV series *Batman*. Brian was a good actor and a team player.

Ten-year-old Danny Bonaduce was a completely different kettle of fish from Jeremy or Brian. Highly talented, he had perfect comedic timing. He was really, really smart and a natural comic. But he was still a kid and would do kid things like get a dish of food and throw it across the room or have a pillow fight. Danny was a wild child who came from an unhappy home. At eleven, he started smoking. At thirteen, he lost his virginity with a girl who visited *The Partridge Family* set one day, searching for David, but ended up with Danny.

Fortunately, Danny respected me, and I used to have him over to my house where he would play with my kids. However, oftentimes David, Susan Dey (who was seventeen and played Laurie Partridge on the show), and I were worried about Danny because of his unhappy home life and talked about him a great deal. But much as we loved and appreciated him, we couldn't deny that he was snotty at times. Once, when he was getting too big for his boots, we all ganged up on him and convinced Susan to pour a pitcher of milk over his head, just to put him in his place. That incident found its way into a subsequent episode of *The Partridge Family*, in which we did exactly the same to David for the identical reason.

Danny also had a hard time remembering dialogue, and once it took him thirty-six takes to get the words right in a scene.

Susan Dey was a teenage model who'd appeared on the covers of *Seventeen* and *Glamour*. She came from Mount Kisco, north of New York Ciy in Westchester County, and was beautiful, naïve —and skinny, but not by accident.

Susan was so dedicated to keeping thin that, during one season of the show, aware that she was now one of the most celebrated teenagers in America, she tried to lose weight by going on a carrot diet. To her horror, her skin turned orange because she ate so many carrots a day.

When she started out on *The Partridge Family*, she had no acting experience. She didn't even know what a close-up was. Her agent was on set constantly, chaperoning her, but that didn't help when she first met David. She took one look at him and fell hard. Later on in the series she even came to me and confided, "I could be so in love with him."

I said, "Well, he is a little older than you and has been around a little more, and he has had lots of girls, so be aware of that."

Nonetheless, Susan tried everything to woo David and, whenever she could, put her arms around him and gave him little hugs, but David manfully resisted her advances. I think he would have had an affair with her if he hadn't been working with her and therefore thought it a bad idea. I agreed with him.

One of the joys of working on *The Partridge Family* was the guest stars. The young Farrah Fawcett had a bit part in the second episode of the show, "The Sound of Money," and everyone noticed what a great looker she was and predicted that she would go on to be a big star.

Ray Bolger, who played the scarecrow in *The Wizard of Oz*, made a guest appearance as my father on the third episode of the show, "Whatever Happened to the Old Songs?" This was one of Ray's later performances, and he couldn't wait to do song-and-dance routines for us between takes. Otherwise, he was a bit irritable and insisted that everything had to be his way.

Jodie Foster appeared on the episode, "The Eleven-Year Itch," (episode 73), when she was only eleven years old, and I thought she was one of the finest child actresses I had ever worked with. She was right on the money with every line. Danny just adored her, and fell madly in love with her.

Dick Clark appeared in the "Star Quality" episode, and I didn't like him very much. But it was great when Richard Pryor and Lou Gossett appeared in "Soul Club," episode 18 of season 1. It was obvious to me that Richard was on drugs the whole time he was working on *The Partridge Family*. He took me to lunch one day and never stopped talking about his life, what he was going to do, where he was going to go, and was so drugged up that he never asked me a thing about myself. In contrast, Lou Gossett was wonderful and we are still great friends today. Rob Reiner was also great when he appeared in the episode, "A Man Called Snake," and was fun to work with, as well.

Some of the episodes in the show were filmed on location. The prison episode, "Go Directly to Jail," was extremely realistic because we shot it in a real prison in the San Fernando Valley. Real prisoners attended our show, and we had to perform in front of them. But luckily they were polite and tame and took pictures of all of us afterward.

In "The Last of Howard," episode 81, and one of the final episodes of *The Partridge Family*, we all went on an actual cruise to Mexico, in steaming temperatures of 120 degrees. Beforehand, I was very nervous about going on a cruise, as I was prone to seasickness, even if I just stood on a dock. So before we started shooting, I underwent hypnosis seven times for my seasickness and, since then, have never been seasick again.

My favorite episode of all was episode 31, "Whatever Happened to Moby Dick?" in which I had my solo "The Whale Song." Everybody loves that song. We shot it in an aquarium and featured whales in the episode, as a way of promoting them.

Making *The Partridge Family* was fun for all of us. In particular, I remember "But the Memory Lingers On," the episode when we discovered a skunk on the Partridge Family bus. They used an actual skunk for the episode, one that we were told had been de-skunked. Unfortunately for all of us, it still sprayed some kind of liquid over us, and afterward, each of us had to sit in a bath of tomato juice to get the skunk stink off our bodies. Not fun at all. Except for one thing: David sang a song called "I Think I Love You" on that episode, which aired on November 13, 1970, and, of course, the rest is history.

As everyone who has ever watched *The Partridge Family* knows, "But the Memory Lingers On" would become the most seminal episode of the entire series, as "I Think I Love You" became a gigantic hit and immediately catapulted David Cassidy to global stardom. Determined to be independent, before he sang the song on the show, he didn't come to me or to his father for any guidance, but sang it perfectly on the first take, and I was extremely proud of him.

After "I Think I Love You" was released, for a few weeks none of the DJs wanted to play it on-air, and one of them even turned down $100 to play it. But it became the biggest-selling record of 1970, selling three million records in the United States and five million worldwide. Before that, none of us had any inkling that David would soon become one of the most famous rock stars in the world, and that America would fall well and truly in love with him.

By the fall of 1970, generally forty or fifty girls a day clustered outside the studio after the show, waiting for David. Eventually, their numbers would swell into the hundreds. David soon began receiving thousands of fan letters a week. He gave his first rock concert in Seattle and was paid $8,000 for it. As he gyrated all over the stage, eight thousand kids aged seven to seventeen screamed with passion for him. Eventually he was making $50,000 a concert and had become so much more popular than Elvis Presley that Elvis actually asked his agent at William Morris who David Cassidy was.

Patrick and Ryan were happy about David's and my being on *The Partridge Family*, but Shaun came on set a couple of times and often asked why he couldn't appear in an episode as well. Neither Jack nor I wanted our kids to go into show business, but to get an education instead, so at that stage, we refused to let Shaun take part in the show.

Starting the week of October 31, 1970, and for sixty-eight weeks after that, *The Partridge Family Album* remained on the *Billboard* pop charts. When Susan and Danny joined David in Cleveland for the Thanksgiving parade there, they were mobbed by eighty thousand people.

Sadly, at the time when David and I started working in *The Partridge Family* together, and David's career hit the heights and he attained instant stardom, Jack's career was downward spiraling. Too many of the Broadway shows in which he'd appeared had closed early, through no fault of his own, and he was feeling a failure and all washed-up.

As David became an overnight sensation, Jack's bitterness reached a crescendo. Perhaps his helping David so much at the start of his acting career only embittered Jack more when David failed to follow Jack's advice and become a jobbing actor and became a rock star instead.

When David became the rock star of the century, Jack was the prophet of doom, telling him, "Rock stars blaze, but then they burn out very quickly, and if you follow this route, your career will be over in a year."

David was making hit record after hit record and didn't want to hear it. Without actually saying it to Jack, David made it eminently clear that he was cleaning up financially and becoming a bigger star than Jack ever was—or ever would be.

David assumed that Jack's attitude was purely motivated by jealousy, but in the end Jack was right. He prophesied that David would end up with money, but that would be all he would have. And Jack was ultimately vindicated.

As *The Partridge Family* soared in the ratings, and David went on to sell twenty million records, he would grow to hate and despise what he was doing.

TEN

C'mon, Get Happy

In the beginning, I was slated to be the star of *The Partridge Family* and to sing every number, but David quickly and easily upstaged me. I was happy for him and didn't mind. If *The Partridge Family* had been my first gig, perhaps I would have minded immensely, but it wasn't, so I was fine with David becoming the star. My only complaint was that I didn't get to sing much in the show, but otherwise I was content that I could spend so much time with my real-life kids and also be in the show.

Meanwhile, David was tasting the fruits of his spectacular overnight success. After his fame reached fever pitch, girls stalked him morning, noon, and night, and naturally he often took sexual advantage of them. I would see one girl go into his dressing room at lunchtime and see her leave a little while later, only to be replaced by another girl. And so it would go for most of the day. I didn't say anything because, as far as I was concerned, David was an adult, and this was his life, not mine.

Despite all the temptations and the sheer number of willing women surrounding him, David did manage to have a serious relationship while making the show. Actress Meredith Baxter, who was three years older than David, met him when she made a guest appearance on *The Partridge Family*, whereupon she and David started dating. She was only recently divorced from her first husband and had two children.

From the first, David was discreet about his relationship with Meredith, but he confided the details to Susan Dey and me. Neither David nor Meredith wanted the tabloids to find out about their relationship, so they evaded them by mostly spending their time in Meredith's nearby Burbank house, where they had a great time together.

The course of true love might have run smooth for Meredith and David, but after they had been dating for about a month, David had a kidnap threat. The FBI broke the news to him, and from that moment on, his life was turned upside down. The result was that his relationship with Meredith faded, then died.

Around the same time, Meredith was cast in a new series, *Bridget Loves Bernie*, along with David Birney. She and David Birney fell instantly in love with each other. That turned out to be extremely tough for my David as *Bridget Loves Bernie* was filmed in the studio next door to where *The Partridge Family* was being filmed, and David was constantly forced to see Meredith and her new man together, making it patently clear that they were so much in love. Eventually, they married.

Before David and Meredith broke up, she confided in me how she thought David was wonderful. She said that he was always a perfect gentleman and never talked about his romances. I knew that David cared deeply for Meredith, even though girls were still throwing themselves at him continually. I knew that he sometimes still caught them, too.

Throughout the series, Susan Dey continued to be crazy about David, but he didn't handle her emotions for him particularly well or sensitively. Often, he would come back from his weekend rock concerts and tell her stories about how he had to get security guards to hide him from all the female fans. He would also tell her about all the ones from whom he didn't hide and the great sex he'd had with them. Susan listened and gave a good impression of accepting the situation stoically, but I knew how hard it was for her because I knew exactly how she felt about David.

Finally, I took him aside and told him that he had to be careful talking to Susan because he was hurting her badly. At first, David didn't understand. I think he may have viewed Susan as the sister he had never had, but I saw the situation differently. She had a great big crush on David, and he didn't reciprocate her feelings. But she wouldn't listen to my advice to stay away from David, and I found myself warning her over and over against getting involved with him. I began to realize that I was sounding exactly the way Sari had when she'd tried so desperately to warn me about Jack all those years ago.

And David was Jack all over again.

During the series, girls besotted with David would come to visit him in Los Angeles, and some of them ended up on my front lawn. They traveled from all over America, and most of them took the train or the bus, as they were too young to drive. I'd wake up in the morning and find one or two of them sleeping on my front lawn.

So I'd go out and talk to them, and they would jump up and say, "I've come all the way from Iowa, and I really want to meet David!" Or "I want to move in with you and have you be my mother and David my brother." Or "I want to join your band and travel around the country in the Partridge Family bus with you and David and the rest of the family."

I'd patiently explain to them that David didn't live at my house, and that he had his own place, and that *The Partridge Family* was a fantasy, not reality.

I felt so bad for those kids. They were so crushed, so disappointed, that their dreams didn't become reality. But I felt worse for their parents and how worried they had to be about their daughters.

"Do your parents know you are here?" was my inevitable first question to them.

The girls would invariably shake their heads, miserable. "I called them along the way and told them I was coming to see David," they would say.

"Well, you must go right home again because this is TV, this is make-believe and not real life. David doesn't live here, and we don't have a band." I would say in a kind but firm voice.

Then I would call the parents and put their minds at rest that their daughters were safe, and next I would buy the girls a ticket home, and the parents would later reimburse me.

Afterward, I felt bad for the kids who genuinely believed that *The Partridge Family* was real, that I was the mother, had five kids, and we were all in a band together. I had to set them straight, sure, but *The Partridge Family* did indeed have a grain of truth. The writers often came over to my house and spent the day with me and the kids and took notes nonstop. What happened in our family might become the theme of a *Partridge Family* episode.

One time, when Patrick was about six or seven, he went to the store and took some candies, just as I had taken bubble gum all those years ago in Smithton. When I found out what he'd done, I reacted much the same as my mother had and ordered him to take the candy straight back to the store and apologize to the owner. That incident became a *Partridge Family* episode.

Sometimes the show seemed so real to me that even I lost track that it wasn't. One time, when Danny was acting up, I lost my patience and yelled, "Danny, go upstairs to your room right now and don't come out till I tell you!"

As Danny cracked afterward, he wasn't really my kid, I wasn't really his mother, and we were on a studio set, not in a house, and there was no room upstairs for him to be banished to. It was funny, but it was also indicative of the way in which the show insinuated itself into my life and mind many times.

The Partridge family had now become America's favorite family. Fortunately, not everyone in the country knew exactly where the kids and I lived in real life. Not that their ignorance always protected us. One time Ryan was out playing in front of the house when a tourist bus pulled up. Out jumped one of the tourists, clutching a "Map to the Stars' Homes."

Did Ryan know the address of any stars' homes? Better still, did he know any stars?

Ryan said, "I sure do. I live with two of them! Park your bus and come on in."

A whole busload of people came tramping into our house. I didn't have the heart to punish Ryan, but I wasn't happy about what he'd done.

Generally, though, the public continued to find

it hard to separate the Partridge family from the real-life actors playing them, which could sometimes cause serious problems in our lives. Poor Evelyn Ward, David's real-life mother, suffered so much because the public persisted in believing that David was my son, not hers. David tried so hard to dispel the rumor and regularly referred to her as his real-life mother in magazine and newspaper features, and during TV interviews to try and make it clear to the general public that Evelyn was his mother, not me. But no matter how hard David tried, and so did I, even today some fans still believe that he is my son, not Evelyn's.

Early on in the series, I could tell that David was suffering from becoming an overnight teen idol. He is sensitive and always craved privacy, and now he didn't have a hope in hell of retaining his privacy. Everything in the show revolved around him. He was the star of the show, a rock god, and one of the most famous performers on the planet. He was spending most weekends appearing in rock concerts all over the country, as well as filming the show all week. The wholesale adulation, the mass hero worship—it all soon became too much for him.

He was burning the candle at both ends, and his schedule inevitably took its toll on his work on *The Partridge Family*. Every Monday there would be a read-through of the script and then we would block the show. On Tuesday through

Friday we would shoot the show. The days would start at seven thirty—except on Monday, when the show started work at ten—and we wouldn't finish till seven at night. Afterward, many nights, David would go straight into the studio, where he recorded till midnight.

Most Fridays, he would board his own plane, fly to a venue, and perform in front of up to seventy thousand. It all took a toll on both David and the program.

After he was an hour late for one Monday-morning reading too many, I took him aside and said, "Listen, I know you are busy working and making money and doing well and I am happy for you, but you can't keep coming in late for the Monday-morning reading. You're a major part of the show, and none of us want to wait for you. Do your thing on the weekend, star in rock shows, but do your part in the show on Monday morning. And be on time."

David gulped. "Okay, Shirl."

He was never late for the Monday-morning read-through of the show again.

Away from the show, David's career continued to skyrocket. On March 11, 1972, Jack and I and the kids went to see his New York concert at Madison Square Garden, where he performed in front of more than twenty thousand fans, and it was incredible. He strutted and swaggered and had a presence onstage rather like Elvis did. He sang all *The Partridge Family* songs and the audience absolutely loved him, although Shaun and Ryan were terrified by the screaming. David was great, and his dancing and singing, brilliant.

After the concert, to escape the fans screaming for him, David was bundled into the trunk of a Toyota, wrapped in an army blanket, and the car whisked him away to Queens, where he hid out in some cheap motel, with no money, and no family to keep him company.

Every single day of the series, David had to be smuggled in and out of the studio, otherwise crazed fans would have torn him apart. Women turned up at his house 24-7. At a restaurant, he couldn't take a mouthful of food before someone would come up pestering him for an autograph. Unhinged girl fans would write him love letters, some full of wild threats, telling him that they were going to turn up and see him face-to-face. Once, two girls hid in his trailer for almost twenty-four hours, then jumped out just as he had taken his clothes off and was stark naked. Girls routinely hid naked in his dressing room, and he had to move houses a couple of times because of fans' mobbing him in his own home.

When he toured Europe in 1973, he flew in his own ninety-nine-seat Caravelle jet. *The Partridge Family Album* had just been released in England, and thousands of fans mobbed him at Heathrow Airport. After he checked into the Dorchester on

Park Lane and the fans found out he was staying there, as many as fifteen thousand of them besieged the hotel, then camped out there all night singing all the Partridge Family songs at the top of their voices.

But things went badly wrong after he performed before forty thousand fans at White City Stadium in London, in 1974, and fourteen-year-old Bernadette Whelan was killed in the crush.

David felt dreadful about that. He felt personally responsible for what had happened, and in a way, Bernadette's tragic and untimely death permanently soured him on being a rock star. It soured him on starring in *The Partridge Family*, as well. The day would come when he would throw in the towel and run away from the show, the rock music, everything. The pressure on him was so heavy that he started seeing a psychiatrist.

Apart from worldwide David Cassidy mania, it seemed that *The Partridge Family* phenomenon, too, was unstoppable. An issue of *TV Guide* in 1972 referred to the Partridge Family brand as "practically a branch of the US mint." Twelve Partridge Family paperback novels had been published, there were Partridge Family paper dolls, real Partridge Family dolls, Partridge Family diaries, David Cassidy lunch boxes, and a Partridge Family collection of clothes. There was even a Partridge Family game.

By the end of 1971, the show was being seen in

Central America, Chile, Colombia, the Caribbean, Brazil, Japan, Thailand, Spain, Portugal, Iceland, England, Peru, Zambia, New Zealand, and Australia, and by 1972, also in Arab countries and in Greece.

By then, *The Partridge Family* magazine was selling four hundred thousand copies a week, and the David Cassidy fan club had two hundred thousand members. To top that, he was nominated for a Golden Globe, although he didn't win.

By the third season of *The Partridge Family*, David had become the rock star of the century, but that wasn't making him happy. He became disgusted with singing what he termed "bubblegum songs" and wanted to go on to bigger and better things and sing hard-rock music in earnest, much in the style of his heroes Eric Clapton and Jimi Hendrix. So he decided to leave the show.

If he had asked my advice, I would have told him to be happy with what he'd got, because that was my philosophy of life. (Besides which, I hated hard-rock music.) But he didn't discuss the subject with me and decided to leave the show.

There was no replacement for him because David *was* the show. We were all sad, but we were also aware that it was just a matter of time before the show was canceled anyway. For some unknown reason, in 1975, ABC had scheduled us against *All in the Family*, which was an edgy adult hit, and *The Partridge Family*, which was primarily made for kids, didn't have a chance to win the ratings battle against it.

Throughout 1972 and 1973, our third season, we had been on top of the world. We had tied with *The Waltons* as the nineteenth most popular show that season.

But during our fourth season, from 1973 to 1974, our numbers started to tumble dramatically.

March 23, 1974, was the last broadcast of *The Partridge Family*. I was sad to see the show end. If it hadn't been canceled, I would have been happy to carry on playing Shirley Partridge for another four years. For me and all the rest of the cast, this was the end of an era.

Just after the wrap party, David took Susan Dey out for dinner. As he said afterward, he fondly imagined that they would stay friends forever. After dinner, the two of them went for a drive together and reminisced about how they'd first met when she was an inexperienced actress, and they both started crying.

Afterward, David put Susan in touch with Ruth Aarons, who became her manager, and also with Lenny Hirshan, his agent at William Morris, who became Susan's agent. For a few years after the show ended, David and Susan stayed friends. She went on to make a great success in *L.A. Law*, in which she appeared as Grace from 1986–92. By then, she and David had grown apart, and nowadays they are completely out of touch, which hurts David tremendously. I was also hurt that out of everyone on the show, only Susan consistently refuses to take part in any TV reunions of *The Partridge Family*.

As for the rest of the cast, Brian Forster went on to study zoology and became a professional race car driver. Suzanne Crough, who played Tracy Partridge, went to college and afterward ran a bookstore; and Dave Madden became a great success in the sitcom *Alice*.

For a time, David and Danny Bonaduce became best friends, and Danny opened for David at some of his concerts. But because Danny sometimes didn't show up on time, David stopped using him. Nowadays Danny has his own radio show and is successful in his own right.

I wasn't mad at David for leaving *The Partridge Family*, but for some reason we hardly talked to each other at the wrap party. Afterward, he took a year off, went to Hawaii, and hung out on the beach, playing his guitar and chilling out. In retrospect, I realized that he'd earned his time alone and time in which to savor his freedom from all the fame and fortune that had been showered on him so suddenly.

I had no regrets about my time on *The Partridge Family*. David and I had worked together on *The Partridge Family* for four and a half years, for sometimes as long as twelve hours a day. During that time, we got to know each other pretty well and grew closer, which was wonderful, and that closeness endures to this day.

The Partridge Family was a marvelous experience for me, not only as a hit show, but because it gave me so much time in which to focus on my boys.

Sadly, though, the stratospheric success of the show took its toll on my marriage to Jack.

As the months went by and *The Partridge Family* became an American phenomenon, and Shirley Partridge became America's favorite mother, Jack embraced the role of Norman Maine to my Esther Blodgett of *A Star Is Born* even more whole-heartedly than before. Not that he was ever suicidal like Norman Maine, but his overriding sense of inferiority in the face of my success drove him into the arms of other women even more often than before.

One night, at the height of the show's success, I was having cocktails at Café Escobar with my good friend Betty Cantu and her husband, Fred, when all of a sudden Jack walked in with his arm around a beautiful young girl and the two of them sat down in a booth on the other side of the restaurant.

As they did, Jack never once took his eyes off his beautiful companion for long enough to notice me. Seeing my husband so enthralled with a young and beautiful girl (who I knew was currently working with him on a show) just tables away from me was devastating for me. I froze.

Betty, Fred, and I were sitting in the booth nearest to the small stage, on which a three-piece mariachi band along with a pianist strumming show tunes were performing.

Observing my shock and anger at seeing Jack with another woman, Fred Cantu leaned across the table and said, "Shirley, why don't you get up onstage and sing a song, just to see how Jack reacts?"

Almost like a sleepwalker, I got up onstage and in a whisper introduced myself to the band, and they struck up the song I requested, "It Had to Be You."

The moment I sang the first line of the song, Jack looked up and blanched. But—in quintessential Jack Cassidy fashion—he retained his sangfroid and carried on chatting extremely flirtatiously to the young girl with him. So I launched into a second song, "Blue Moon."

But I had also been drinking and was so upset that I threw caution to the wind, stormed off the stage, and stalked over to the booth where Jack and the girl were sitting.

"Fancy meeting you here, Jack. Just one of

those things, is it?" I said, alluding to one of the songs we loved to sing together.

Jack didn't bat an eyelid and calmly said, "Shirley, this is—"

"I don't care who she is."

I stormed out of the restaurant.

To my surprise, Jack finally lost his fabled composure and rushed out of the restaurant after me. Right there, on the pavement in front of the restaurant, I let loose. For one of the few times in our marriage, I let him have it. "You son of a bitch!" I screamed.

But even though he'd been caught red-handed with another woman, Jack wasn't about to admit anything and immediately spun me a risible story about the girl and why he was having dinner with her. She wasn't just an actress, he said. She was also a secretary and had just finished helping him with some correspondence. Afterward, he said, she claimed to be starving, and he had taken pity on her and invited her for a quick dinner at Café Escobar. And so on. I knew he was lying, so I just walked away from him and went home on my own. Then I did my best to calm down and put aside my anger, so that when he came home a short while later, I didn't mentioned the incident to him or ever refer to it again.

In my heart, I did believe that the Café Escobar incident meant nothing to Jack, and that the girl he was with really was "just one of those things," another girl in a long line of girls with whom he dallied briefly, then discarded.

At the time, *The Partridge Family* was on hiatus, and Jack and I were considering touring in our own show, *The Marriage Band*, a musical celebration of marriage, which took a couple through their first meeting, their wedding, their first child, and finally their harmonious life together.

Some irony . . .

In January 1972, out of the blue, Jack asked me to have a pizza with him at a little local Italian restaurant. I'll never forget what happened next.

With little preamble, he announced, "I think we need a separation, Mouse."

I genuinely thought I'd misheard him. "A separation? Did you say we need a separation? But why?" I said, fighting back the tears.

Jack shifted in his seat. "Mouse, I need to live by myself right now. I don't want a divorce. I just need to be by myself. I just can't be here for the kids and for you anymore. It's an age thing," he said lamely.

I blurted out the first thing that sprang to mind. "So is there another woman, Jack?"

Jack shook his head. "There is not," he said adamantly. "I just think we ought to try a separation and see what happens."

At that point, we had been married for fifteen years, and despite Jack's eternal craving for attention, his lack of jealousy, his excessive drinking, and his constant infidelity, I truly loved him and was happy with him. I was devastated.

"I don't understand, Jack, but if that's what you want, fine," I managed to stammer, after a while.

"Just give it time, Shirley."

I choked back my tears and left the restaurant, alone.

I only lost control when I arrived home and burst into floods of tears. Then, for some inexplicable reason, I switched onto a strange type of automatic pilot. I took down all the scrapbooks of our life together, put them on the dining-room table, and kept adding more and more new pictures to them. I pasted picture after picture into the album as the tears coursed down my cheeks.

Jack had followed me home a little later, and by the time I had stopped crying, he was in his office, crying his heart out, as well.

He said, "I'm moving into an apartment, but I don't really know why."

"You have to do what you want to do," I said.

Soon after, on January 15, 1972, Jack did move out. The kids were angry with him. David stopped talking to him altogether. My mother, though, said, "I feel sorry for you, but maybe it is a good thing." She'd always hated Jack.

I knew Jack was living in an apartment in Hidden Hills, but neither I nor the kids ever visited him there. Then he called and told me that he was going into therapy and suggested that I do, too. So we both went to see the same therapist, only separately. At the end of the therapy, I didn't feel as if I'd received any lightning bolts of wisdom.

But I did learn that the moment I had started to grow up, Jack had been unable to handle it and probably never would.

ELEVEN

When You Walk Through a Storm

When Jack, out of left field, broke the news to me that he wanted us to separate, I was still appearing in *The Partridge Family*. All my friends and all the cast members knew that I was separated from Jack and were kind and supportive to me.

Soon after Jack left me, out of a sense of self-preservation, unhappy as I was, I started dating. I met the father of one of Patrick's friends, a divorced amateur tennis player, who was so proficient at the game that he could have turned professional. We ended up in bed together at the Beverly Hills Hotel, and the sex we had together was nice. Later on, he bought me some jewelry, nothing expensive, but nonetheless a warm and loving gesture. However, our relationship quickly fizzled out. Then I met an attorney and dated him for a while, but after Jack, I found him boring.

I was yanked out of my boredom, though, when I discovered that Jack had lied to me all along. A friend of mine told me that he was living with Yvonne Craig, the actress who'd starred as Batgirl in the TV series *Batman*. (She had also once appeared on an episode of *I'm Dickens, He's Fenster*, with Marty, who had not been immune to her charms.) Yvonne Craig was young, innocent looking, and overt about her sexuality. Voluptuous and sensual, she also combined the qualities of a siren with those of a little girl.

But not that little a girl . . . she had been romantically linked with Elvis Presley, Mort Sahl, and Robert Vaughn. Yvonne and Jack first met when they appeared together in the *Love, American Style* episode "Love and the Big Game," which aired on January 29, 1971. At the time, Jack didn't even mention her name to me.

To top the hurt and indignity of discovering Jack's liaison with Yvonne Craig, to my fury I also discovered that before he moved in with her, he had been paying the rent on her luxurious apartment. All that in a time in which he was not making a great deal of money and, as always, I was supporting both of us. Finally, I confronted him, and he confessed the truth. He hadn't wanted to tell me, he said, because he hadn't wanted to hurt me. Which, of course, was ridiculous.

Soon after, Yvonne left Jack as a result of his accidentally running over her dog in the driveway and killing him—or so the story went, according to Jack. He was never able to be alone, so now he wanted me to take him back. I didn't have to think too long about my answer. We had three children together, he was their father, and despite everything I still loved him.

The psychiatrist I was then seeing told me that I was making a big mistake by taking him back: "You are never going to change that man. Don't go back into this marriage thinking you can."

He was right, of course, but the Shirley Jones who had fallen so deeply in love with Jack Cassidy so many years ago wasn't prepared to relinquish her dream man. And I didn't. So after eight months of separation, Jack and I reconciled on August 29, and he moved back into our home.

One of the by-products of our separation and reconciliation was that our always-hot sex life became even hotter than before. It seemed that absence had made the heart, and other organs, fonder—for both of us. Which, perhaps, explains what Mrs. Partridge did next.

The Partridge Family was on hiatus again, and Jack and I started touring in *The Marriage Band*, the show that he had written and produced for us, a musical anatomy of marriage.

We played the Cocoanut Grove, various theaters in the round, and as the show was spectacular, with sixteen singers and sixteen dancers, it was perfect for Las Vegas and was scheduled to open at the MGM Grand Hotel there.

I had become friends with one of the dancers

in the chorus, a girl whom I'll call Jean. She was slim, pretty, with dark hair, tall, boasted the classic dancer's body, and was not busty. I wasn't threatened by her because Jack adored big bosoms in a woman more than anything else. As it turned out, he was prepared to drop this particular preference when a woman really appealed to him. Or was prepared to do anything to please him.

So one night after the show, Jack turned to Jean and said, "Honey, come and have a drink in our suite with us." I wasn't the least bit surprised. Jean was a nice girl, and we both liked her.

But nothing in my previous life or my marriage to Jack could have prepared me for what happened next.

The three of us sat around, drinking and talking. Jack and I drank Scotch and water, and so did Jean. I was relaxed, happy, and when Jack leaned close to me and kissed me passionately, I kissed him back passionately. Then he turned to Jean and kissed her passionately as well.

I'd been drinking, so I didn't go into shock. Almost in a trance, I watched as Jack started taking Jean's clothes off. To my amazement, she seemed to be all for it.

In retrospect, I wouldn't be at all surprised if she and Jack had planned what would transpire between the three of us that night.

"Mouse, now you take your top off, as well," he said.

I did, and he kissed me again, almost as if rewarding me for stripping off my clothes so readily in front of Jean. Then Jean moved closer to Jack, and he hugged her. Then the three of us hugged.

The next thing I knew, we were all in bed together. A thought flashed through my mind: "This will please Jack. And who knows, maybe this is something I should try. Maybe I'll enjoy it."

Jack started directing the two of us. "Kiss Shirley, Jean."

She did, and I let her. I'd never kissed a woman before, and Jean's lips were far too soft for my liking. But I went ahead and kissed her right back. I had never fantasized about having sex with a woman before—nor would I ever do so afterward—but that night I was willingly engaging sexually with another woman just to please my husband.

At the back of my mind I was sure that Jack had been to bed with Jean before, and that he'd planned this, going to bed with both of us at the same time. I didn't get the slightest sense that night that he was in love with Jean.

Consequently, when he gave her oral sex, I felt that he was taking part in a physical exercise—which he was thoroughly enjoying—but nothing more than that. I didn't want to scratch Jean's eyes out, and I didn't feel competitive with her, either. I wasn't jealous or insecure. I just sat and watched.

After a while I started wishing that the entire enterprise were over.

Then Jack took Jean's hand and put it between my legs. I lay back while she masturbated me, and I had an orgasm. Having orgasms had never been that difficult for me because I was always very sexual and easily turned on, so that night in Las Vegas with Jack and Jean was no different.

Meanwhile, Jack carried on directing us. "Isn't this fun? You are going to feel so good about this, Shirley."

Jack, Jean, and I spent three hours in bed together, going through all the various permutations of lovemaking . . . although perhaps that's the wrong word. Love had nothing to do with it —it was just sex. To Jack, having sex was just like eating a slice of pie: part of his life, and meaningless. For all I knew, he had probably already had sex with all the other dancers in the show, as well. Until now, I had looked away.

But now I was in bed with one of them.

As dawn was breaking over the Strip, Jean said, "Good night. It was a lovely evening. I really enjoyed it," and then she left. Afterward, Jack and I hugged, then we fell asleep in each other's arms.

The next morning, Jean came up to me and whispered, "I hope you weren't too embarrassed about last night. I really apologize if it was a bad night for you."

I shook my head. "No, Jean, it wasn't."

Jack was in the seventh heaven about what had happened. "Jesus, Shirley, isn't Jean a great girl?"

I nodded and said nothing because I interpreted his comment as meaning that Jean was a great girl to have around for sex but for nothing else. I was his wife, he loved me, and I knew that Jean wasn't for him. But what the three of us did together that night wasn't for me, either. Jack knew it, and he intuited what I was about to say before I said it, which was "Jack, I love you, and I want to be with you, but I don't much enjoy having threesomes with you."

If Jack hadn't fully come to terms with my sexual boundaries before, after that night in Las Vegas with Jean, he now understood conclusively that threesomes were just not my thing. From then on, I assumed that he went his own way, sexually speaking, and, I guess, had threesomes with other women instead.

I was still madly in love with him, and my awareness of his many infidelities, in whatever permutations he chose, didn't tarnish my love for him. Nor did our threesome with Jean. She stayed in the show, and we remained friends and never ever talked about our night with Jack again.

Soon after, I was back on the set, Shirley Partridge incarnate, and America's favorite mother.

Off camera, in the real world, the Swinging Seventies were in full bloom, and Jack was determined to explore every aspect of the new sexual freedom. He wanted it all: swinging, pornography, drugs, group sex. I carried on just looking away and ignoring his infidelities. But when all the stress of his career failures, the drugs, the wild nights, and the multiple sexual partners started to take their toll on him, I had to confront the horrendous truth about what was happening to him.

After he first came back to me after our separation, I couldn't help noticing a change in him. I knew he was drinking too much, taking too many drugs, as well as receiving "vitamin shots" from a Las Vegas doctor. Forever afterward, I wondered what was in those shots but never found out.

Jack had always been the consummate professional, but now he sometimes forgot his lines onstage and instead started ad-libbing wildly, leaving me confused about my next line or my next move. He started taking sleeping pills at night and then pep pills in the morning, and once or twice, to my shock, he actually missed a show altogether.

One night, when we were playing a theater in Warren, Ohio, he went out to get some cigarettes (by then he had a four-pack-a-day habit). After about an hour, he arrived back at the hotel and came up to the suite again. He walked through the door and then slammed it hard behind himself, dramatically. I saw that his eyes were glazed over and that his hands were shaking involuntarily. Then, in a hushed voice, he said, "I just had a long conversation with my mother."

Jack's mother had been dead and buried for years. I was speechless.

He went on in a rush of words, "I met her on the street on my way back here. She was standing under an old oak tree in the square, and I stopped and talked to her. We had a long conversation. She warned me to be very careful of my smoking. She said that my cigarettes were going to kill me."

At the time, I placated Jack and didn't pay any attention to his words. I dismissed his mother's supposed warning that Jack's cigarettes would end up killing him. I only remembered that "warning" years later, when one of Jack's cigarettes did ultimately kill him. By then, of course, it was too late.

For years, Jack felt his career hadn't ever hit the heights of which he had dreamed. He had starred in Broadway shows, but many of them closed far too soon—and not because Jack gave a substandard performance. Jack never did that. Through the years, he guested on episodes of *Cheyenne*, *Wagon Train*, *Alfred Hitchcock Presents*, *Maverick*, *Hawaiian Eye*, *Bronco*, *The Real McCoys*, *77 Sunset Strip*, and *Surfside 6*. But he never became the star he wanted to be.

Along the way, he was offered the part of Ted

Baxter in *The Mary Tyler Moore Show*. The part had, in fact, been written specifically for Jack, but, perhaps because it came too near the truth about himself—who really wants a mirror held up to themselves?—he made the rare error of turning the part down. Later on, though, he did a guest shot on an episode of the show, which aired on October 23, 1971, in which he played the part of Ted's twin brother, Hal, a photographic model.

Despite turning down *The Mary Tyler Moore Show*, he was now a regular guest on TV quiz and talk shows and had established a strong presence on television as a witty *bon viveur*, playing himself really. But despite his success on television, he continued to yearn to conquer Hollywood.

When he was cast as the villain in Clint Eastwood's thriller *The Eiger Sanction*, I was intensely relieved. Jack was finally on the threshold of the movie success he had craved for so many years. I hoped against hope that perhaps this new upsurge of his career, and the possibility that he might now find Hollywood success at last, would put his emotions and his life on an even keel once more.

However, since we were still touring in *The Marriage Band* and had to play our last series of shows at the MGM Grand in Las Vegas, I hadn't reckoned on his having to commute to *The Eiger Sanction* location in Death Valley every day. So he was forced to get up at five each morning, then rush to catch a helicopter, fly to Death Valley, work on the movie all day, then fly back to Las Vegas in time to go onstage with me at the MGM Grand. A tough schedule, and in retrospect I believe he paid a high price in his health, his nerves, and his entire mental stability.

One night, soon after he had flown back from Death Valley, and we were both supposed to be getting changed to go onstage, I walked into the living room and found Jack crouched in the corner of the room, stark naked.

We had to go onstage in half an hour, so I stayed as calm as I possibly could and explained that we needed to do the show.

Jack met my gaze serenely, then said, "I finally know now that I'm Jesus Christ."

It flashed through my mind to say that Jesus probably never played cabarets, but I stopped myself from making a joke.

Then Jack fixed me with a hypnotic gaze and launched into a rambling monologue, which ended with "Shirley, my father is here. My mother is on her way. I have to speak to them. So lock yourself into your bedroom, as I am not sure what I am doing."

I couldn't deny to myself anymore that Jack was seriously mentally ill. And that right then he was in the middle of a nervous breakdown, with all that entailed. I had no choice but to admit the truth. Mindful of his warning, and aware of the dangers in staying around someone in a manic stage and capable of harming himself and anyone in his vicinity, I followed Jack's advice and took refuge in my bedroom, and the lock clicked. Jack had locked me in.

I picked up the phone and called our business manager, Howard, in LA and gave him a blow-by-blow account of Jack's bizarre behavior, ending with my considered opinion that Jack was in the throes of a full-blown nervous breakdown.

I explained to Howard that I didn't want Jack to be carted away to a hospital here in Las Vegas, but that I wanted him to be transported to a Los Angeles hospital. Howard assured me that he understood my feelings and that he was primed to leave for the airport at once and would fly to Las Vegas straightaway and bring Jack back home to Los Angeles with him.

Moments after I hung up with Howard, Shaun called. "Don't worry, Mom, we'll come and get Dad."

I was intensely touched by his concern and his offer of help in this crisis. But I told him that he needn't come himself. Howard was on his way and would take Jack home.

By now, the enormity of the situation had hit me, and I was crying my heart out, shaking and begging Jack to open the door and let me out of the bedroom, but to no avail.

Within an hour, Howard, who had had the

presence of mind to rent a private jet, arrived at the suite. But Jack refused to open the door. However, I could hear Howard pleading through the door with Jack, begging him to get dressed and let him take him back to LA.

"Shirley can do the show on her own tonight and carry on that way till you've served out your contract," Howard explained to Jack in as conciliatory a way as possible.

That pulled me up short. Jack might be in the midst of a nervous breakdown, but that didn't mean that the world had stopped dead. We still had a show to do, and like any actor, I knew without a shadow of a doubt that the show always has to go on.

So after Howard managed to gain admission to our suite and opened the door for me, I went onstage and announced to the audience that Mr. Cassidy was unable to perform that night due to illness. "The show is about love and marriage," I said, "and it was obviously written for two people, not one. So I hope it won't seem funny that I'm singing both parts."

Then I did half the show (rather than struggle through all of it) on my own. Fortunately, the audience was completely unaware of the sad events that were occurring behind the scenes and seemed to love it.

Later, I learned that Howard had literally picked Jack up, thrown a robe on him, got him to the airport, and then onto the plane. According to Howard, Jack didn't protest, but was still in a manic state and all during the flight kept saying, "My mother is up there. The plane is going to crash because she's going to bring it down."

Then he switched tacks: "That spider over there! That's really my mother. She's been reincarnated as a spider, I swear!"

Jack's madness had a strange kind of logic as his mother was named Charlotte, as is the spider in *Charlotte's Web*. And she had certainly spun a web of guilt around Jack. When he was a child, she had beaten him severely; consequently his relationship with her was always strained, and he did not attend her funeral. Hence the guilt, which, I believe, was partly responsible for his psychotic episodes.

When he got back to Los Angeles, thankfully he agreed to seek medical treatment for his mental health, and I hoped against hope that the treatment would work, but sadly it did not.

One evening toward the end of 1973, I came home one night after appearing in a concert, to find that Jack had lit blazing fires in every fireplace in the house, each of which was piled high with wood. He kept throwing more and more wood and paper on the fires, and the resultant heat was unbearable.

The moment he saw me, he immediately took his pants off and said, "Let's make love." Petrified by his state of mind and wanting to placate him, I followed him into the next room, where he threw more wood onto the fire in the fireplace there, then ran out of the room and threw more wood onto every single other fire in the house, as well.

I begged him to stop, but he wouldn't. So I followed him back into the bedroom, terrified of what he would do next. And what he did next was horribly predictable, given Jack's highly sexed nature. He lay down in front of the bedroom fireplace, where the flames were blazing sky-high, and began to masturbate. I just stood there, watching, paralyzed. When he finished, he threw more and more wood into the fire, then more paper, just like a pyromaniac. I was terrified. In contrast, Jack seemed riveted by the roaring fire, mesmerized by the spectacle he had created.

"Isn't it beautiful! Look how peaceful the flames are! This is the way we should all be!" he murmured.

Then he tore off again to fetch more wood to add to all the fires burning in the house. I was frightened in the extreme, convinced that at any minute he would set the whole house on fire, with both of us and our boys asleep in it.

The thought of Shaun and Patrick and Ryan yanked me out of my terrified stupor. By now it was two in the morning. I snuck out of the room when Jack had his back to me as he continued to throw yet more paper into the fire. He was so intent on what he was doing that he didn't notice that I'd slipped out of the room. In another room, and in a whisper, I called my psychiatrist, Dr. Rosengarten, and gave him chapter and verse on what Jack had done, what he was, even now, doing.

Highly alarmed, Dr. Rosengarten told me to sit tight and remain exactly where I was at that moment. "I'm calling an ambulance," he said.

With my heart in my mouth, I went downstairs, just in time to see Jack arranging wads of paper all around the coffee table, obviously planning to set the coffee table alight any second. Thankfully, before he could strike a match and create an inferno right there in our home, the ambulance screeched to a halt in our driveway and out jumped two orderlies carrying a straitjacket. Seeing them, Jack stood rooted to the spot. As they moved to start strapping him into the straitjacket, the shock of what was about to happen to him caused him to suddenly snap out of his mania.

Now acutely aware of what was going on around him, that he was being strapped into a straitjacket, Jack fixed me with a look so terrible that, even today, I still can't erase it from my memory and said, "Mouse, are you really going to let them do this to me? Are you really going to let them take me away?"

I was lost for words and stood back as the

orderlies led Jack into the ambulance. Just as they were about to close the door and drive off with him, he yelled out of the window, "Shirley, I'll never forgive you for this."

As the ambulance roared off toward Westside Hospital, a private psychiatric hospital, I doubted that he ever would.

Over and over, I asked myself if I had done the right thing. But I truly believed that I had had no choice. Yet I completely understood Jack's anger toward me and his sense of betrayal, and I could hardly forgive myself for what I'd done to him. But looking back, I believe that I didn't have a choice. If I hadn't called the ambulance that night, Jack might well have become so unhinged that he might have set our house on fire, with our sons in it. Their lives had been in danger from Jack's rash actions, his mental illness. I knew I had had no other choice but to have him taken away.

To this day, I am still haunted by the sight of the man I'd loved and lived with for a greater part of my life, the father of my children, the man whom I worshipped and adored, being led away in a straitjacket like a wild animal.

That night, the doctor and I traveled in a car following the ambulance, and at the hospital I was compelled to sign the papers committing Jack to the hospital for treatment.

His psychiatrist arrived soon after and gave

me his diagnosis that Jack was manic-depressive, which nowadays is known as bipolar. We now know it to be a condition suffered by many tortured geniuses, but back then it was a terrifying diagnosis. The doctor said that he planned to put Jack on a dose of lithium to control his bipolar episodes.

Jack remained hospitalized for three days at Westside Hospital, and I was by his bed constantly, watching over him, but he still raged against me, refusing to utter a single word to me.

After seventy-two hours, according to the law, Jack was able to check himself out of Westside Hospital. He moved into a motel and refused to take the lithium that had been prescribed for him. Perhaps he didn't want to accept the doctor's diagnosis that he was bipolar, but his avowed reason for not taking the lithium was that he hated the idea of taking drugs. I was too upset to remind him that he was hardly a stranger to taking drugs.

Finally, he must have come to terms with his condition, as he checked into Cedars-Sinai Hospital and spent two weeks there, working with a psychotherapist. He started taking his medication religiously, but still carried on drinking, which was a lethal combination.

While he was at Cedars-Sinai, he and I talked every day, and slowly, very slowly, the ice between us began to melt. I even began to hope that we still had a chance to forge a new and better life together.

But after two weeks, Jack checked himself out of Cedars-Sinai and flew to New York, where he moved into one of the best and most expensive hotels in Manhattan and started spending money as if there were no tomorrow.

Of course, there was no tomorrow. Not for our future together.

The truth about the man I loved, and about our marriage, was penetrating my consciousness at last, so that I finally started to come to terms with the harsh reality that my life with Jack, my dream man, my white knight, my sexual Svengali, might well be ending forever.

TWELVE

And Don't Be Afraid of the Dark

Against all the dictates of my heart, my emotions, in November 1974 I filed for divorce from Jack. However, he didn't accept my decision. In the six months before the divorce became final, he repeatedly begged me to reconsider, to take him back. You don't stop loving someone whom you have loved for eighteen years, but I knew in my heart that I could no longer risk my emotions and, more important still, the safety of my children by staying married to Jack. His mental state meant that allowing the children to be around him was to risk their lives. So although Jack and I had separated before and reconciled, I held firm and refused to rescind the divorce.

I was heartbroken at the end of my marriage to Jack, but all the odds had been stacked against us. Besides, by then I had met another man who was becoming increasingly important to me, comedian Marty Ingels.

On February 3, 1976, in response to Jack's letter

begging for us to reunite, I wrote him the following letter:

Dear Jack,

Your letter moved me and moved every emotion that I possess. As your words always did in the past. I know it took a lot of soul-searching for you to write it. You asked me for an answer but perhaps there hasn't been enough searching on my behalf to give you an honest or direct one. You said you had grown up in the last year, well so have I. It only made me realize how much growing I have to do.

In the beginning I thought my life was over with you, and I guess it was. Nothing helped, not even our three children, who through it all had survived very well. And I hope have few scars.

Then I did pick up a few pieces and put them back into place even stronger than before and I had the help of a wonderful kind man who made me laugh and gave of himself totally in every way.

You said one becomes more cautious and less vulnerable with age and growth and that is certainly true with me. I don't mean I have lost the willingness to give. But it doesn't come as freely or as willingly. I think I am happy now but not totally fulfilled. But then I don't know if any of us can expect that to come out of life. I think we came close to total happiness at many times and I live on those memories too. But at this time in my life I can't go back to living on a memory.

It's not enough for me, Jack, I don't think I can continue to live my life without Marty, because as I said at the beginning of this letter everything is day-to-day existence. But I know I want to keep it this way for now.

I will always have love in my heart for you, Jack, and thoughts for you daily. And who knows what the future will hold. Your children will always be there for you if I have any say about it and if you continue to want them. And I will be there for you if you ever need or want me. But I can't live side by side with you. Be happy and content, dear Jack. You deserve it.

Love,
Shirley

I continued my relationship with Marty, and Jack began dating actress Lois Nettleton. But we still had three children together, so we remained in contact, despite everything.

In November 1976, Jack and I met for dinner at a local restaurant, ostensibly to talk about the kids. Patrick was doing well at school, in particular in sports, and longed to have his father come to some of his games. True to form, Jack always said yes to everything but never showed up.

So we talked about the kids, and then Jack stopped short and said, "Are you happy with this guy?"

He had never mentioned Marty by name, and this time was no different.

I told him that I was.

"I'm glad," he said. Then he asked me if I would come and see his apartment, as I'd never been there before.

I was wary because I sensed that he would try to get me into bed for old times' sake, but I agreed to go.

Once we arrived there, he made me a drink, and I sat down in a chair opposite him, out of his reach.

Then he held out his hands to me. "Shirley, I still love you, and I want you to come back. I can't imagine being without you for the rest of my life. You belong with me. This is the last time I shall ever ask you to come back with me, but we belong together."

In some ways, I still felt the same about Jack, but deep down I knew that there was no hope for us. I loved Jack deeply, but I was no longer in love with him. He was in so much pain, and I felt for him so much, but nevertheless I knew that we could never again live together.

"Jack, I still love you, and I always will, but I've got someone else now." I stood up. "I've got to go." I felt lost and alone, yet certain that I was doing the right thing.

As proud as ever, Jack didn't try to stop me from leaving. Instead, he stood up, took off the beautiful blue scarf he was wearing around his neck, and placed it around mine.

Then we hugged.

And I left, choking back my tears.

Jack Cassidy, the only man in my life whom I'd ever truly loved, the grand passion of my youth, was in such bad shape, so sick, so alone, and yet I had to face that I could no longer help him or be with him.

While I cried for his pain, and for both the sadness and the happiness of our past together, I knew that that past was now well and truly behind us, and our life together was over.

On December 11, 1976, Jack called me one more time. It was Patrick's birthday on January 4, and Patrick wanted a particular brand of bike as his birthday gift. Jack and I chatted for a while about that, and I asked him to do his best to be at Patrick's birthday party so that he could give the bicycle to Patrick himself. Jack said he would try.

I knew that he would. But bitter past experience had taught me that it was doubtful he would succeed, and that inevitably Patrick would once more be disappointed by his father.

"Shirley, I've got the tree up. Why don't you

come over and have a Christmas drink with me," Jack suddenly said.

I sensed that he didn't intend for us just to have a Christmas drink together, but that he hoped against hope to be able to turn back the clock once more.

"I can't, Jack."

"You mean you don't want to?"

I didn't answer.

"Don't you understand, Mouse? We had what dreams are made of," he said after a long silence.

Those were the last words Jack Cassidy ever spoke to me.

"I know that, Jack. I think about it all the time," I said.

And I still do.

At four in the morning on December 12, I received a call from my manager's secretary, who lived on the same road as Jack. Without any preamble, he broke the news that Jack's apartment had been gutted in a raging fire. A body had been found, but the burning heat had melted the person's jewelry and burned the face so that it was charred beyond recognition and no one could identify it.

We all knew that Jack had had a friend staying in his apartment because Jack intended to drive to Palm Springs that weekend with Lois Nettleton. And Jack's car, a classic silver Mercedes convertible, was still in his garage. So all of us, me and Jack's sons—David, twenty-six; Shaun, eighteen; Patrick, fourteen; and Ryan, ten—hoped against hope that the charred remains did not belong to Jack.

Of all the boys, at this point Ryan was closest to Jack. Sadly, Jack and David were no longer talking. But as soon as David learned the tragic news of the fire and heard of the possibility that the charred remains might be all that was left of his father, he rushed over from his home in Beverly Glen.

He was crying when he arrived. "Oh, my God, it can't be him, it can't be him."

Later in the day, after dental records were checked, and the gold signet Cassidy-family-crest ring was found near one of the burned fingers, we learned, without a shadow of a doubt, that the charred corpse was, indeed, that of Jack Cassidy.

As the news sank in, David held Shaun and Patrick and Ryan in his arms, and the four of them, Jack Cassidy's four sons, all held one another and cried. At that moment, David said later, he felt his father's spirit surge through him. And he felt that Jack had not lived in vain. He had created all four of them, and now they were united, as one.

The police pieced together what had happened to cause this horrific inferno that led to Jack's tragic and untimely death. On that night, the night on which Jack had invited me to come to his apartment for drinks, the invitation that I had refused, Jack went instead to Dominick's, his favorite Italian restaurant on Beverly Boulevard, right across from Cedars-Sinai Hospital, for dinner by himself.

Eyewitnesses at the restaurant claimed that Jack had spent the evening with two men, and that at the end of the evening he left the restaurant with them. The police were never able to establish the identities of those men. I even tried to do that myself, as I wanted to interview them, so that I could find out what had happened during the last hours of Jack's life. But I was unable to find them, or to discover who they were and the nature of their connection with Jack. To this day, their identities remain a mystery to me and to the boys.

All we knew is that Jack was drunk when he came home that night, that he lay on his Naugahyde couch, smoked a cigarette, then fell asleep. In his sleep, he must have dropped his cigarette onto the couch, and the couch exploded in flames. Jack was burned to death.

Horrifically, in the eleventh hour, he must have woken up, seen the blaze all around him, and started crawling to safety. But blinded by all the smoke and flames, instead of moving toward the apartment door to the corridor and safety, he lost all sense of direction and crawled toward the balcony instead. Which is where his body was found, on the floor, facing the balcony.

At the time of his death, Jack was only forty-nine years old—which, in an eerie coincidence, was exactly the same age at which my father had passed away. At least Jack had died knowing that his career was at last on an upswing. He had been nominated for an Emmy for his role on the TV production *The Andersonville Trial*, he had costarred with Paula Prentiss in the series *He & She*, and he had finally just recently made two extremely successful movies, *The Eiger Sanction*, with Clint Eastwood, and *W. C. Fields and Me*, in which he played his idol John Barrymore.

So David, Shaun, Patrick, Ryan, and I could at least take comfort in that Jack had died seeing his dreams of movie stardom on the verge of fruition. He had also been constantly haunted by his fear of growing old and aging visibly. But now, of course, that was not to be. Yet however much I tried to console our sons and myself about Jack's death and to focus on the positive, it was incontrovertible that Jack had died far too soon. His death was so unnecessary and so sad.

Four hundred people, including Milton Berle, who had first worked with Jack when he was only eighteen years old and they were both appearing in *Spring in Brazil* on Broadway together, attended Jack's funeral at the Chapel of the Pines in Westwood Memorial Park. Toward the end of the ceremony, I stood up and talked to the mourners about the Jack Cassidy I had known, about our marriage, our life together.

I began, "Jack was an extraordinary man with an uncanny sense of humor and a gifted talent. He was one of a kind and the world suffers a great loss that he was taken from it so soon." I ended by repeating Jack's very last words to me: "Don't you understand, Mouse? We had what dreams are made of." In many ways, we did.

No matter how happy I am with Marty today, and despite that we have now been together for more than thirty-six years, both Marty and I know the truth: *I still love Jack Cassidy, and I will carry on loving him until my dying day.*

After Jack's death, all his sons had to come to terms with his memory and his legacy in general. They remembered his charm, his great talent, but were bitter when strangers accosted them on the street and raved about Jack's star quality. Where were they when Jack was out of work and struggling? the boys wondered.

They remembered their father for his positive qualities, his hard work and professionalism, his grasp of the business, and his bursts of unexpected generosity. For example, when David was about eight years old, Jack suddenly went out and came back with an eighteen-inch TV for him. At that time most small boys didn't have their own TV sets, but Jack gave one to David, and for a while David was considered the coolest boy on the block.

The boys also couldn't help remembering the

more negative aspects of Jack as a father. There were his fits of rage and his angry shouting in a theatrical voice so loud, so strong, that the boys trembled in fear when they heard it. And then there was his drinking. David remembered going to dinner with Jack one night and watching as he downed no less than seventeen glasses of Scotch and soda!

They also remembered that he was always skilled at creating toys and furniture, and in particular at building train sets to scale. One Christmas, the boys were thrilled that he had built an intricate railroad, just for them. Except that the boys never got to play with it, not once. Jack did, though, over and over, and never let his sons go near it.

Even when the boys were just children, Jack was always virulently competitive with them. When he was married to Evelyn, she always complained that whenever he wrestled with little David, although David wasn't even seven years old, Jack never let him win.

With hindsight, I now realize that Jack was such a child himself that he could never let his children have their time in the sun or allow them to eclipse him in any way, because, to Jack, the limelight belonged to him and only him.

Apart from having divorced him, my crime, in his eyes was to have taken some of the limelight from him. I was not surprised, when Jack's will was read, to discover that I was no longer in it. He left Patrick and Ryan and Shaun $50,000 each, but David was not left anything. He and Jack had been quarreling bitterly around the time that Jack wrote out his final will.

But nothing could deprive either David or Shaun or Patrick or Ryan of the positive elements of Jack's heritage: the charm, the good looks, and the talent. Nor me of the happy memories of my life with Jack.

Flashback to the summer of 1974. Jack and I were on the verge of divorce, a divorce that, although I accepted it intellectually, I was still unable to accept emotionally. I was depressed, feeling lower than I'd ever before felt in my life, and all of a sudden Marty Ingels crashed into my world. Literally. Though I was in the midst of one of the worst periods of my life, I had reluctantly agreed to attend an art exhibition in aid of a worthy cause that was to be held on the front lawn of Michael Landon's Beverly Hills house.

Given my black mood, I didn't intend to linger at the exhibition. I said a brief hello to Pat Boone, to James Garner, and to Betty White, who were all on hand to support the art sale, then I spent the minimal time viewing the pictures. As soon as politeness decreed that I could slip out without causing too much of a fuss, I made my apologies and left. As I walked toward my car, Marty hared around the bend and bumped straight into me.

He apologized profusely, then introduced himself. I've always had a weakness for comedians, and I knew exactly who Marty Ingels was—the Brooklyn-born star of the sitcom *I'm Dickens, He's Fenster*, and a very funny man indeed. But like so many comedians, his great sense of humor cloaked a hidden sadness, and I knew that he had had a nervous breakdown right on prime time, during Johnny Carson's *The Tonight Show*.

That day, until then a bad day in a bad week in a bad month in a bad year, for both of us, Marty threw me a penitent smile, and his large brown eyes twinkled at me. All of a sudden, much against my will, something deep within me was triggered. So I threw him back a smile, accepted his apology, and moved on toward my car.

As I did, Marty yelled after me a stream of words that tumbled out at the speed of lightning. A little unnerved, I kept on walking and only paused for a second to yell back, "Later, Marty, later." Then I got into my car, drove away, and didn't give Mr. Ingels another thought.

Although I didn't know it at the time (and if I had, I might have been alienated by Marty's obsessive nature and relentless will to win, no matter what), Marty spent the next six weeks trying to get in touch with me. Aside from that, he also devoted his every waking hour to researching my life and my career in libraries all over town.

He also assembled a mountain of photographs of me and created a collage out of them.

His persistence in trying to find my telephone number finally paid off. He slipped a secretary at my agent William Morris's office $20 to get my phone number for him, and she did.

After that, he showered me with telephone calls, all taken by my maid, none of which I intended to return. Then one day when I was particularly depressed and had spent most of the day driving around LA aimlessly, I answered the phone myself. Marty was on the line, and I listened, amused, as he introduced himself again and asked me out to dinner.

I thought for a second and decided that it might be worth spending an evening with him, as he might be good for a laugh. Before I had time to respond yes, Marty launched into an intricate, rambling speech, which I later discovered he'd spent weeks crafting and polishing, and he made me a love declaration about how he longed to present me with a flawless corsage and to escort me to the prom, how he felt about me, and a myriad other prepared charming sentiments. In the end, I cut in and said, "If all this is a prelude to asking me out to dinner, the answer is yes."

Stunned to receive the answer he'd been longing for, Marty still didn't want to be diverted from his prepared speech. "I just have one more paragraph to go. Shirley, would you mind if I finished it?" I tried hard not to laugh and said that I wouldn't mind at all. And he finished reciting the last of his speech: more charming sentiments, more clever comments. Once again, I was both amused and beguiled by him.

From that moment on, till the present day, Marty has never really gone away. He was now in my life, and he was there to stay. Despite that practically everyone close to me—my friends, my family, fans, and even strangers—thought that I shouldn't be with him, not even for an hour, never mind married to him for an entire lifetime.

Part of the problem, I suppose, was that when Marty and I first met, although I was separated from Jack, Jack was still very much alive and in the public eye. To the outside world, glamorous, dashing Broadway star, matinee idol Jack Cassidy was streets ahead of Marty Ingels in every aspect. But the outside world didn't get the measure of Marty from the moment they first met him, as I did. And the outside world didn't get to know him as well and as quickly as I did, or to fall in love with him almost from that first meeting.

So that while everyone else—even to this day —asks himself, and other people, what I see in Marty, and why, ultimately, I chose him over Jack, this is my answer: Both men and women adored Jack. But not as much as Jack adored himself. Marty's major problem was always that he didn't have any self-worth. In contrast, Jack had too much. Besides, what the world doesn't see is that Marty has always taken good care of me.

On a less positive note, through the years I've learned that one of Marty's primary qualities is that no holds are barred with him, but the good thing is that you know exactly who he is the first moment you meet him. He craves attention constantly and will do anything to get it. He is bright, but because he is a comic and yearns for applause, he wants to come over as crazy. He likes to be underestimated by everyone.

Unlike Jack, who would have died rather than display any jealousy toward the many men who attempted to woo me, Marty has always worn his heart on his sleeve. Emotional self-control is alien to him; so is tact and subtlety. But I don't mind. I'd rather know what I'm getting into. That way, I can be sure that there will be no hidden surprises.

Talking about surprises, two of the many things the disapproving world doesn't know about Marty Ingels: he is a magnificent dancer, and more to the point, he is also a great lover. He was never as sexually oriented as Jack was—but that was just as well, because Jack's high-octane sexuality meant that he indulged in sex with everyone under the sun, whereas Marty is a one-woman man.

He is also extremely romantic. After we first met, I was making the TV movie *Winner Take All*, in which I played an alcoholic gambler (a part I loved), and filming took place in various locations all over town. Marty bribed an executive at Universal, which was producing the movie, to slip him a copy of the shooting schedule.

He then rented a thirty-eight-foot motor home and, every morning at eleven, drove to one of my favorite restaurants, the Brown Derby, in Hollywood, and picked up my favorite Cobb salad, and a bottle of vintage champagne.

Then he drove the motor home to wherever I was filming that day, waited for the lunch break, then got out of the motor home. Imagine my surprise to see him standing there, dressed in a pure-silk smoking jacket with an ascot round his neck, ready to lead me into the motor home, where he would serve me a candlelight lunch with my favorite song, "An Affair to Remember" (from the Cary Grant/Deborah Kerr film of the same name), playing romantically in the background.

After he learned that my favorite color was green, he presented me with a dozen green carnations, accompanied by a photograph of himself, which he'd had tinted green!

When he discovered that I was dating a producer, a much older man, he flared up in jealousy. But never one to suffer in silence, the scent of competition set his competitive nature ablaze. And—although, to this day, I can't work out how he managed this—he snared copies of the producer's various X-rays from his doctor's office. And I don't mean of his teeth. Of every single organ in his entire body—his bones, his muscles, everything!

After which, Marty went to work. He pieced together all the various X-rays, so that they formed a picture of the producer's entire body, and pasted it onto a large card. Then he painted large arrows pointing to health problems from which the producer was suffering, from gout to sterility to ulcers. Then he had it delivered to me, anonymously, complete with a note informing me that, given Mr. Producer's health, there wasn't much point in planning a future with him.

Another time, years later, on one of my birthdays, Marty threw a party for me at a Hollywood restaurant and, beforehand, placed a red phone next to where I was going to sit. Little did I know that he had devoted weeks to researching every aspect of my past and had called everyone who had touched my life through the years.

Consequently, all evening, at prearranged fifteen-minute intervals, the phone would ring and a voice out of my past—Ralph Lewando, my aunt, a cousin in Canada, a friend whom I hadn't seen for twenty years—was on the line, primed to wish me happy birthday. All because Marty had taken the trouble to contact them and arrange for them to call me on this very special evening.

During our courtship, my past with Jack sometimes reared its head, particularly while Jack was still alive. One time, soon after Marty and I first started dating, while we were away together on a romantic trip in San Francisco, Jack showed up at my apartment in a moving van and somehow let himself in and removed many pieces of my furniture, including the bed and the credenza, and many of my paintings.

True, he had selected the furniture and remodeled it and had alerted me to the beauty and the value of the paintings and the antiques. So he simply assumed that it was his prerogative to reclaim ownership of them and went right into my home and took them, just like that. I didn't mind too much. I understood Jack's reasoning. Besides, I never cared about possessions. Marty, however, was incandescent with rage, and I did my best to mollify him.

Unlike Jack, Marty was always an arch romantic. Whenever I went to his apartment, he always placed my favorite flowers by the bed and had my favorite music playing in the background. None of Marty's overt romanticism meant that he was averse to moments of rampant sexuality, though. One night, he took me to see an erotic movie at the drive-in theater, and when the lights went up, he looked at me, I looked at him, and we rushed home and had sex right there on the floor of our living room.

Of course, Marty can be difficult, but he can also be extremely charming. And he's never ever boring. On our first date, he picked me up in a motor home. On our second, he booked a luxurious hotel suite and ordered a gourmet dinner for the two of us to be served directly on the stroke of nine, only for us to arrive at the door of the suite and find it barred. Apparently, his credit card had been declined on suspicion of fraud.

Ever resourceful, Marty switched to another hotel and talked himself into a suite by invoking the name of his uncle Abe Beame, who had been mayor of New York.

Like many creative, mercurial geniuses, Marty always had psychological demons to fight. Ten years ago, he was diagnosed as bipolar, just as Jack was before him. Strange, I suppose, that I ended up marrying two men who were bipolar. Then again, I was never attracted to the norm. I guess I always wanted someone who was the opposite of me.

If anyone still wonders why I married Marty Ingels, this quote from Marty himself is my answer: "Who would be my dream woman on Valentine's Day? I would get Linda Evans and Daryl Hannah and Joan Collins, put them in one room, lock the door, and go and have dinner with Shirley. Shirley is the world to me."

Marty truly feels that way about me, and believe it or not, I feel exactly the same about him and always will.

On November 13, 1977, Marty and I were married in a beautiful ceremony held at the Hotel Bel-Air.

Our new life together began in earnest at last.

THIRTEEN

The End of the Road

By 1977, Shaun had followed in David's foot-steps and become a rock star, and it was Shaun's turn to be in the spotlight, but he didn't much like it. Even as a child, he was shy, an artistic loner who preferred to paint or watch TV than play with his school friends.

Out of all my sons, Shaun is more like me, rather than like Jack. Shaun is definitely a Jones, as opposed to being a Cassidy. From the time that he was a small boy, he was always his own person and followed his own path in life.

When he was six years old, I gave a huge party for him and his friends in a park, complete with pony rides and long tables filled with hot dogs and cakes. But the moment Shaun arrived at the park, he turned to me and said, "Mom, I want to go home now."

"Why, Shaun? This is your birthday party and all your friends are here."

"I want to go home now, Mom."

I didn't take him home, I made him stay at the party, but he obviously hated every minute of his own birthday party.

As Shaun grew older, and less shy, unlike David, who was always seriously intimidated by his father, Shaun never was. By the time he was thirteen, he had morphed into a complete rebel who refused to listen to his father at all. Despite Jack's oft-expressed disapproval, Shaun kept his hair shoulder-length and practiced for his rock band each night at full blast.

When Shaun was older, Jack and I were worried by the bad influences he might encounter growing up in Beverly Hills. So Jack decided to take Shaun out of Beverly Hills High School and, in the hope that he would grow up more normal by going to school in a more normal environment, send him somewhere more stable. So Jack found Shaun a private school in Bucks County, Pennsylvania, instead.

Poor Shaun was unhappy there and years afterward said, "Mom, you don't know what kind of a place you sent me to. And you thought Beverly Hills High was bad!"

In fact, I did have an idea pretty soon after Shaun started there that the school in Bucks County wasn't exactly a hotbed of virtue. One time, a couple of guys from there turned up at our house in LA. They both seemed sinister, and one of them ended up in jail on drug charges. We took Shaun out of that school after just a year.

When Shaun went on to become a rock star, he hated every minute of it. He could sing, and he liked performing, but he always loathed what came with it. Beforehand, we warned him about the pitfalls, but he just shrugged them off by saying that he had witnessed what had happened to David and wouldn't fall into the same traps. David was the main reason Shaun became a rock star; he admired David so much that he followed in his footsteps. So Shaun, too, had a great career as a famous rock star from 1977 to 1979. Ruth Aarons became his manager and he had three platinum albums and five hit singles, including his album *Shaun Cassidy*, which went multi-platinum and led to his number one single, "Da Doo Ron Ron," plus a Grammy nomination for Best New Artist.

However, despite his stratospheric success, Shaun was extremely uncomfortable as a teen idol. Completely immune to the glamour of being adored by millions and having a vast fan base, Shaun ran away from all the attention most of the time. Whenever we ate out at a restaurant and fans gathered in front, Shaun would beat a hasty exit out the back door. He just didn't like the adulation and the lack of privacy.

He had another great success when he appeared in the TV series *The Hardy Boys/Nancy Drew Mysteries*. Fortunately for him, Jack had mellowed to such a degree that early in Shaun's career, he actually went so far as to tell him that he was proud of him. And so was I.

In 1977, I played Laura Talbot, a murderess in the TV movie *Yesterday's Child*, and had to smother a child, which was extremely difficult and unpleasant for me. Of course, the "child" was actually a doll, but I had a hard time smothering it all the same!

In the seventies, I took on a new and different gig as the spokesperson for the Sunbeam company (which manufactured home electrical products), promoting their products on the road, and did that right through the early eighties. This big deal paid extremely well.

Until the early eighties, I'd never been tempted to be unfaithful to Marty, but while I was promoting Sunbeam products, I was on the road a lot and, during that time, had a flirtation with a good-looking sales representative.

He came up to my hotel room, and we exchanged a few passionate kisses. He was ten years younger than Marty, and awfully attractive, but although he wanted to come and visit me when I was staying in my cabin in Big Bear, all alone, I refused to see him. I confessed everything to Marty and he understood and forgave me.

In 1979, I was excited to get my very own series, *Shirley*, in which I played Shirley Miller, a widow with three kids (including a daughter played by Rosanna Arquette) living in a farmhouse in the country, where I was inundated with men who wanted to date me. A terrific premise, I thought, and I had great hopes that *Shirley* would be as successful as *The Partridge Family.*

Television executive Fred Silverman, who created *All in the Family*, *The Waltons*, and *Charlie's Angels* and had only recently been made president of NBC Entertainment, was the producer of *Shirley*, and he was highly encouraging, forever telling me how fabulous I was, and how wonderful the show was, after it debuted on October 26, 1979. Then, after we'd made thirteen episodes, I arrived at the studio bright and early one morning, ready to start recording the next episode of the show, and was told point-blank that the show had been canceled. No warning, nothing. Not a single word from Fred Silverman. Classic show-business behavior; everyone is all over you when you are successful, but woe betide you when you aren't! I just hate that. Which is why, when all is said and done, I prefer animals to people.

Soon after *Shirley* was canceled, Marty and I were having dinner at the Polo Lounge in the Beverly Hills Hotel when, all of a sudden, I noticed that Fred Silverman was having dinner in one of the booths along with three women.

I turned round to Marty and said, "That asshole! I'm going to go over to him and tell him exactly what I think of him!"

Marty went chalk white. "Please, Shirley, please don't do that."

I calmed down, we finished our dinner, but as we were leaving, I strode straight over to Silverman's table and gave him a piece of my mind. "You acted like you were my best friend, but you never said a word to me when the show was canceled!"

Silverman was speechless while I raged on. "And why was the show canceled, anyway?" I stormed.

"I . . . I tried to get in touch with you," Silverman spluttered.

"Sure." I stalked away.

Leaving Silverman in shocked silence.

Marty, who had never before seen me in one of my more forthright moments, said, "Are you crazy, Shirley?"

For once, it was my turn to be the crazy one in our marriage and take Marty utterly by surprise! And I was glad.

In the eighties, like many mothers, I was compelled to grapple with the tragedy of drug abuse. Ryan, always a frail and asthmatic child, had become addicted to marijuana and to cocaine. In retrospect, the signs were writ large: he started sleeping for most of the day, then staying out for most of the night. His school marks plummeted; so did his attendance. And Marty discovered that more than $2,000 was missing from his cash box. Only months later (when we had established that Ryan was taking drugs), after much probing on my part, did Ryan finally admit that he had stolen the money to fuel his drug habit.

Long before Ryan made his confession to me, Marty and I suspected that he might be taking drugs. But whatever our suspicions, Ryan wasn't admitting anything, and we did not have conclusive proof. Only when Patrick came by one night and, with our consent, searched Ryan's room, did we find evidence that he was doing cocaine. The Jack Cassidy habit of substance abuse had been handed down to his son Ryan, and I was devastated.

Marty did extensive research—one of the many things at which he is excellent—and, in November 1985, unearthed an innovative rehab center in another state far from California. The program offered there was for a year, and during that time Ryan would be banned from communicating with the outside world. Which, of course, included me. As the ultimate non-Jewish Jewish mother, the prospect of having all communication between me and my beloved youngest son severed was unbearable. But I knew that if Ryan was to beat his drug habit, I had to cut him loose from my apron strings and give him the chance to save himself.

Four days after Thanksgiving, an emotional time of the year under the best of circumstances, Ryan and I flew across the country together to the rehab center. When I met the director of the rehab center and he gave me further information about the program and what lay in store for Ryan, I almost grabbed Ryan and took him straight back to the airport. But I knew I had to keep strong for his sake. So I gritted my teeth and said good-bye to him. Soon after, his suitcase was shipped home to our house, full of Ryan's belongings, even his toothbrush, as the rehab center dictated that he could bring nothing with him from his own home.

Once inside the facility, Ryan's head was shaved and he was consigned to sleeping on the floor in a dormitory. Later, he would graduate to sleeping in a bunk. All in all, the psychology behind this rehab center mirrored that of the military: tear a new recruit down, then build him up.

Ryan was allowed no contact with his family, and when I committed the grave offense of writing to him myself, my letters were sent home to me, unopened. According to the rehab center's strict rules, I wasn't even permitted to speak to my son on the telephone.

However, the rehab center's director did take my calls, and we talked continually, updating me on Ryan's progress. After five months, the management made an exception, and I was allowed to see Ryan at last.

The moment I set eyes on him, I was unnerved. He was rake thin, his head was shaved, and he was smoking heavily. He reminded me of a prison inmate. He never stopped talking and almost seemed high. I was terrified, but reluctant as I was to leave him, I returned to Los Angeles with a heavy heart.

Ryan remained at the rehab center for another thirteen months, then Patrick, who was deeply concerned about him, flew out to see him. When Patrick arrived, he didn't like the condition in which he found Ryan and swore on the spot to take him home right away.

Problem was, Ryan wanted to be true to his pledge to stay the course at the rehab center and didn't want to let down his friends there by cutting, running, and abandoning them. But Patrick's mind was made up. This particular rehab program wasn't good for his brother, and Patrick was taking him home with him, no matter what.

Ryan resisted Patrick's pleas to leave the center until, in the eleventh hour, shortly before his plane was due to take off, Patrick told Ryan that his car was waiting outside, and that Ryan ought to leave with him. Ryan plucked up his courage and informed the man in charge that he was leaving. He was going home. As he did, every single resident in the place turned his back on Ryan in disdain.

As Patrick told us later, Ryan then trudged upstairs to his room, but once he got there had to crawl on his hands and knees to get his belongings, as residents were forbidden to walk upright around their own bunks. Then he threw everything into a trash bag, picked it up, and followed Patrick into the car.

When Ryan's plane landed at Los Angeles airport, we were all there, waiting for him. As he deplaned, I saw immediately that he had undergone an immense change. His hair was in a crew cut, his clothes were torn, and he looked for all the world as if he had been in a combat zone.

Once Ryan arrived home, he went from room to room, touching everything, the tears running down his cheeks as he did. When I think of that day, I can't help crying myself.

Since then, I am so happy to say, Ryan has been clean.

In 1988, I sang "God Bless America" for President Reagan at the last night of the Republican National Convention. The occasion was moving, and I was honored to be singing for the president. At the same time, I couldn't help remembering one night at Chasen's with Jack, many, many years before.

Ronald Reagan was then president of the Screen Actors Guild, he was having dinner that night at Chasen's, as well. Later on that evening, he and Jack ended up in the men's room at the same time.

Jack, who'd known Reagan for years, said, "How are you doing, Ronnie?"

"I'm doing dreadfully, Jack. I've got no work, and I don't think I'm ever going to work again. It's terrible."

"Oh, I can't believe that, Ronnie" was Jack's heartfelt reaction.

Jack came back to the table, told me the story, and, although he liked Ronnie, noted, "He probably isn't the best actor in the world."

Jack was probably right, but now Ronald Reagan was president, and here I was, singing for him. Afterward, I slept in the White House, in a bedroom adjoining Reagan's playroom, which housed his pinball machine, and which was decorated with pictures of the movie stars with whom he'd worked.

That same night in the White House, Nancy Reagan came up to me and said, "You and I started in Hollywood at the same time. Look what's happened to you!"

I glanced around the White House. "Look what happened to *you,* Nancy!"

In all, I sang for President Reagan three times. Although my family were Democrats, I've always been a Republican. But I also sang for President Johnson, when I performed *Oklahoma!* in a shortened version, which we enacted on the front lawn of the White House. President Johnson had his dogs with him, and we chatted about our mutual love for man's best friend.

The first American president for whom I ever

sang was President Eisenhower. Jack and I sang duets for him and Mamie Eisenhower at the White House, and afterward we joined the president and the first lady for dinner, along with twenty other people. Mamie was funny and bossy. In a way, she made fun of the president, saying, "Stop eating with that fork!" and "Why don't you talk to so-and-so."

After Gerald Ford was no longer president, I attended a reception for him at the Beverly Hills Hotel, where he was staying on his own. Afterward, to my surprise, he came over to me and asked me to dance.

After we danced, to my amazement he said, "Oh, that was lovely! Can you come to my room for tea tomorrow?"

I was nonplussed, but I accepted.

At four the next afternoon, sharp, I went up to the former president's room, nervous about what was about to unfold between us.

But Ford was ahead of me. As he opened the door to the suite and motioned me to sit down at the already-laid tea table, he said, "I just want to talk to you about your career and your business."

We were alone together, and I was still nervous that he was about to make a pass at me. But, true to his word, he just asked me questions about the business. When it was time for me to leave, he simply shook my hand and said, "I enjoyed meeting you. I enjoyed dancing with you. Thank you."

I've also sung for both President Bushes. I sang at the Republican National Convention for the first President Bush, before he was elected president. He was lovely and Barbara Bush was funny, with a great sense of humor.

One time, after a concert, Marty and I went to a party at the Beverly Hills Hotel, and Marty went up to Barbara and said, "Hello, my name is Marty Ingels. I'm Shirley Jones's husband."

And Barbara said, "My name is Barbara Bush. And I'm George Bush's wife. Don't you hate these parties? So boring."

In the seventies and the eighties, Marty carved out two new and lucrative careers for himself. First, he became the world's first celebrity broker, and it happened quite by chance.

It all began in 1972, when an old friend from the army, Larry Crane, called him, begging for advice. Crane desperately needed a big star with a great voice to be the spokesman for his record company.

Marty listened, waiting for the punch line. Soon enough, Larry told him that he was calling from a New York restaurant where, to his intense frustration, for the entire evening he had been sitting at a table opposite the one where the perfect spokesman for his record company was sitting: none other than my old friend Rossano Brazzi, Latin lover supreme, an actor and singer with a perfectly pitched baritone voice.

Marty listened, puzzled. Why didn't Larry just stroll over to Rossano's table, introduce himself, and make his pitch to him, himself? Larry demurred and said that he just wasn't the kind of guy who could do something like that. Marty, however, was born for the job, Larry said.

Marty was hugely flattered, just as Larry had intended him to be, and after hanging up, Marty called the restaurant and demanded to be put straight through to Mr. Rosanno Brazzi, who was dining there. Within seconds Marty was on the line to Brazzi. Without introducing himself or evoking my name or *Dark Purpose*, the movie Rossano and I had made together, he informed Rossano, "I should be awarded a Nobel Prize for having tracked you down here!"

Rossano started laughing, Marty chimed in, and within moments Marty had made the pitch on Larry's behalf, and Rossano had agreed to the deal. Only one problem, Rossano said, where was Marty right at that moment? And who would be giving him his contract?

"After you hang up, a gentleman will come to your table and hand you his card, and that will be the man who will give you your contract," Marty said in an inspired moment of quick thinking.

Then he called Larry back, and at Marty's behest, Larry walked a couple of feet across the restaurant to Rossano, handed him his card, and within a week, Larry had signed Rossano Brazzi to be the star spokesman for his record company. From then on, Larry Crane considered Marty to be the hero of the year.

Over the next few months, Marty repeated his miracle over and over and, at different times, convinced a dazzling assortment of stars, including Bing Crosby, Buddy Greco, Don Ho, Arthur Fiedler, Rudy Vallee, Jerry Lee Lewis, Trini Lopez, and Louis Prima to work with Larry Crane in New York. To Marty, the process was so simple that it resembled taking candy from a baby.

Along the way, he realized that he had unwittingly identified a big gap in the market: companies wanted to hire celebrities to promote them, but most celebrities were protected by talent agents who didn't want to let them out of their sight, never mind make a deal for them to work with a commercial enterprise.

Marty vowed to change all that. With my encouragement, he cleared out one of our bed-rooms and put a desk and two phone lines in it. After *Advertising Age* in New York ran a short feature about Marty and his new celebrity brokering business, his phones started ringing off the hook. Most of the requests were for Marty to link a caller who represented a charity with a celebrity spokesperson.

Although Marty wouldn't be paid by the charities, he went ahead and started working for the charities anyway. He hired John Wayne to work for the Cancer Foundation, Robert Mitchum for the Boys Club, Burt Lancaster to work with UNESCO. On the commercial front, he arranged for commercials for Howard Cosell for Canada Dry, Robert Wagner for Timex, and Orson Welles to make a commercial for Lincoln.

Marty's biggest challenge of all, we both thought, was to convince Cary Grant to narrate a documentary on the American presidency. Unfortunately, Marty never did seal the deal with Cary, but the journey was interesting, and our brief contact with Cary Grant, fascinating.

We invited Cary to come over to our house in Beverly Hills so that we could discuss the potential deal with him in a relaxed, informal setting. But on the day of our meeting with Cary, Marty was so nervous that he didn't think he would be able to say even one word to Cary when he arrived. So he asked me to step in and save the day. I agreed.

Cary appeared, looking as handsome and urbane as ever, and he and I sat on the living-room couch, and Marty sat opposite us. Then our "conversation" began.

"Shirley, would you ask Cary how he feels about narrating the documentary," Marty said.

"Cary, did you hear what Marty asked? He wants to know how you feel about narrating the documentary," I said.

And so it went, like something out of a bad Kafka book. However, for one moment Cary and I did communicate for real. Seeing how handsome he still was, I asked why he didn't still appear in movies.

Cary sighed. "I just don't look like Cary Grant anymore."

There was no answer to that, so I remained silent.

Then we went back to talking about his narrating the documentary. At least, I did, prompted by Marty, with Cary responding. After about half an hour of excruciating dialogue between Cary and me, orchestrated by Marty every step of the way, Cary got up and went into our guest bathroom.

While we waited for him to come out, Marty and I exchanged gloomy glances. This was not going well.

Then Cary emerged from the bathroom, a big grin on his face. "Shirley, Marty, everybody should have what you have in your guest bathroom!"

Marty and I were dumbstuck.

"That hook on the back of the guest-bathroom door," Cary went on. "Wonderful. That way you can take your coat off and hang it up while you are . . ."

After Cary left, Marty had a special sign made and put it under the hook, which read CARY GRANT'S FAVORITE HOOK.

But before Cary did leave, I remember his

turning around and saying, "I hope you both know that, from now on, we are going to be living in a world of plastic."

I didn't know what to say to that, either.

Not booking Cary Grant was one of Marty's few failures in the celebrity brokering business. He connected such clients as Arnold Schwarzenegger, Joan Collins, Muhammad Ali, Joe Montana, and Scott Carpenter to advertisement campaigns, and I was hugely proud of him.

One morning in 1982, Marty was casually fielding a call on behalf of his client Robert Culp. Then Marty was disconnected and called back, but by mistake reached the telephone number of Gordon Hunt, an executive at Hanna-Barbera.

"We've got the rights to Pac-Man!" was the first thing Gordon Hunt said to Marty. Marty was intensely puzzled. What had a luggage company to do with Robert Culp's next job? he asked himself.

So Marty launched into his pitch for Robert Culp, only to have Gordon Hunt stop him in his tracks and compliment him on his voice.

Marty does, indeed, have a remarkable voice, strong, rich, gravelly, and with a marked Brooklyn accent. All of which caused Gordon Hunt to offer him the chance to become the voice of Pac-Man in the cartoon series *Pac-Man*.

The company had already auditioned 173,000 voices for the part of Pac-Man, but none of them had been right, Gordon Hunt explained. But Marty, with his evocative Brooklyn accent, and his comedian's perfect sense of timing, was Pac-Man incarnate, Gordon Hunt declared.

Marty got the job as Pac-Man, and for two wonderful years traveled once a week to the studio in his pajamas, then recorded three weeks of episodes of Pac-Man's voice in an afternoon. He made more money from being the voice of a cartoon character than he had made in his entire career as a comedian. So he gave up his celebrity brokering business, and no longer dealt with a string of Hollywood legends.

Through the years, I've met other show-business legends and have drawn my own conclusions about them.

In 1969, I appeared on *This Is Tom Jones* with Tom Jones and absolutely loved him, but we didn't have an affair. We sang together, both having the last name Jones, both coming from Wales, and when I confessed to him that I had never been to Wales, he charmingly said, "You have to come there. And I'll show you around. . . ." The meaning was clear, but I wasn't in the least bit tempted.

I also worked with Jerry Lewis in Las Vegas. I've always admired him as a performer, and Marty adores Jerry because Jerry gave him his first break in show business. Jerry is a super-duper talent, but I found him far too full of himself.

He would never talk to me the way a regular person does.

I remember when he remarried and adopted his first daughter and I admired her photograph. "Isn't your daughter beautiful!" I said.

"Yes, she's the light of my life, besides my business," Jerry responded.

Other than that, I could never get a straight answer from him about anything. Every conversation always revolved around Jerry, and nothing else. But I still appreciated it that he was always so good to Marty.

Marty was also close to Danny Kaye and adored him, as well. Years before I introduced Marty to Danny, I found out that Danny could be a bad boy. One day I was in a restaurant, wearing a low-cut sweater, when Danny came over and put his hand right on my breast and said, "That's pretty nice. . . . You're a beautiful girl, and I admire you."

"Thank you, Danny," I said, and removed his hand from my breast.

On February 13, 1997, Marty and I did an *Oprah* segment on marriage, along with Marion Ross and her husband. As always, Marty was afraid to fly, so we took the train from Los Angeles to Chicago together.

We did the show, during which Oprah made it clear that she wasn't crazy about Marty and his big mouth. When the show was over, and all us guests walked off the stage, Oprah didn't follow her usual practice and come backstage to talk to us guests. We were all surprised.

Then one of the other guests on the show raised the subject of our fee.

"Fee? What fee?" one of the production assistants said indignantly, before breaking the news to us that Oprah would not be paying any of us for appearing on her show.

"This is Chicago, not LA or New York," the production assistant said, somewhat reprovingly.

None of us guests were buying that we ought not be paid the AFTRA scale of $600 for our appearance on *Oprah*. At Marty's behest, all us guests on that show signed a petition demanding to be paid the AFTRA scale. In the end we were paid, but Oprah never forgave Marty and me, and we were never invited to appear on her show again.

However, I had a great time making three episodes of *The Drew Carey Show*. In 1998, I played Celia, Drew's middle-aged girlfriend, and it was all great fun. According to the script, Drew signs up to get a master's degree at night school and meets sixty-two year old Celia there and starts dating her. Eventually, Drew's parents come over and assume Celia is the maid. Drew asks Celia to move in with him, but then their relationship ends. Drew didn't really act, though. He just played himself. But I loved working with him and playing a "cougar" for the first time in my career.

It wouldn't be the last.

FOURTEEN

There's a Golden Light

In February 2001, Marty and I separated. No third party was involved. I had resisted having an affair with my Sunbeam man, and although Marty had flirted with other women now and again, no one threatened our marriage.

He did have a flirtation with Patrick's first wife's mother, whom he met at Patrick's birthday party. He talked to her for the whole evening, and I could tell that he was hugely enamored of her. The next morning, she turned up at our house and issued an invitation to Marty, asking if he would like to have lunch with her. Fortunately for our marriage, he refused.

Neither of us had been unfaithful, but we still decided to separate. The reason? The ongoing conflict between Marty and my sons David, Shaun, and Patrick. Of all the boys, Ryan was always the most well-disposed toward Marty. Marty, of course, practically turned cartwheels to win him over, and it didn't hurt that Marty showered Ryan with gifts. Consequently, Ryan dubbed Marty "neat."

It was always unbelievably hard for Marty to be a stepfather to my three sons and David. Marty was married once before, but never had kids and was also never a family person. In a way, he understood that he might not be capable of handling the situation.

But stepfamilies are difficult to negotiate—for all stepfamilies. And ours was no easier than others. At first, Marty tried to turn all the boys into his allies and treat them as if they were his friends. Then he switched tack and tried to become an authority figure instead. That didn't work, either. The problems between him and David, Patrick, and Shaun were evident as early on as our wedding day. Shaun gave me away, but David was not there, although he had warmed to Marty on their first meeting and thought he was funny. David was happy that I'd found someone, but Marty quickly alienated him by saying, "Hi, shithead," to him. Marty called everyone that in those days, but David just didn't understand.

Patrick also had difficulty in accepting Marty in the beginning. He was a comic, a big mouth, and Patrick didn't like that kind of person. I also think he felt that Marty was taking financial advantage of me—which was untrue, because when we first met, he had far more money than I did. But I was a movie star and Patrick believed that Marty was influenced by that and didn't really love me. That didn't bother me a great deal because Marty and

I loved each other and that was enough for me.

Shaun also took against Marty, extremely quickly. When Marty and I first got together, Shaun's show-business career was skyrocketing, and he was hardly around, so his relationship with Marty was on hold. Shaun, being true to himself, was always highly outspoken in his feelings about Marty. One of his early comments about Marty was "What the hell is this? What the hell did you marry?"

My answer was and is "I married the man I love. He is good for me, he loves me, and he is kind to me. In fact, he is much better for me than your father ever was."

I never tried to influence Shaun to accept Marty, and Marty was often unhappy that I didn't make an attempt to do so, but I believed that it was futile.

When Shaun got married, he didn't invite Marty to his wedding. At first, I said I wouldn't come without Marty, but Marty suggested that I go anyway. After the wedding, I had lunch with Shaun's new wife, Tracey, and told her that I was happy for her and for Shaun and didn't want us all to be at odds with one another. In the beginning, we all had Christmas at my house, and Shaun and Tracey and Tracey's parents came, but then Marty said something that rubbed Shaun the wrong way, and Shaun said he and his family would never come to our house again. To him,

Marty was too much of a showman, too much of a maniac personality, and Shaun just doesn't like either of those qualities.

But to my joy, this Easter Sunday (which happened to fall on my birthday), he reached out to Marty and invited him to his Easter egg hunt.

He called out of the blue and said, "We'd like you to bring Marty."

I said, "That's wonderful." And although both Marty and I were nervous, wonderful is what it turned out to be.

And I ended up having the best birthday of my life—perhaps the best day of my life, ever. And I am so thrilled that Shaun and Marty are now reconciled and we can all spend time together with Shaun and his family and be happy.

Patrick's relationship with Marty was another story. Patrick was twelve years old when Marty blazed into my life, a difficult age under any circumstances to have to accept a man other than one's father in one's mother's life. Patrick was so unhappy with my new relationship with Marty that, even though Jack and I were then well and truly separated, Patrick often threatened to move out of my house and go and live with Jack again.

I doubted very much if Jack, then living with Yvonne Craig, would have welcomed his twelve-year-old son into his home, but for Patrick's sake, I didn't say as much.

Instead, I always asked him if he had discussed

his decision to go to live with his father with Jack. Patrick always replied yes. Then I always sighed and said that if living with Jack was what Patrick wanted, then that was what he should do. At which point Patrick would always burst into tears and I would hug him and there would be no more said about his moving out.

When Jack and I finally divorced, out of all my sons, Patrick took it the hardest. He couldn't understand the reason for the divorce and made me responsible. I never defended myself because doing so would have meant criticizing Jack to his own sons, and I had vowed never to do that. So I remained silent as Patrick hurled utterly untrue accusations at me like "It's all your fault. You didn't love Daddy enough."

Patrick considered Marty the enemy, and nothing I could do would ever dissuade him. Then tragedy struck. One afternoon in 1975, while I was filming *Winner Take All* in Gardena, Los Angeles, Jack phoned me. Patrick had been spending the weekend with him and, as Jack explained, suddenly complained of severe back pains.

Fortunately, Jack acted quickly and took Patrick straight to the emergency room at Cedars-Sinai Hospital. There, Patrick underwent a series of X-rays, which showed he had a tumor adjacent to his spine. Patrick's medical condition was critical, and an operation was scheduled for the very next morning.

Jack didn't mince his words about the prognosis. "The tumor could be malignant," he said bluntly.

Before the operation, poor Patrick underwent a series of painful tests and procedures, including an injection of dye into his back and a spinal tap. Then he was wheeled into the operating theater.

Jack and I waited at the hospital, terrified the operation would be unsuccessful and that Patrick would be paralyzed, or worse.

Finally, the operation was over. A tumor the size of an orange was removed from Patrick's back. To our relief, the doctors informed us that it was not malignant, nor had it been attached to Patrick's spine. There was no danger of paralysis.

Patrick was moved into intensive care, and Jack and I visited him at various intervals during the day. Soon after, he was moved into a private room.

Then Marty, who, at Jack's behest, had not been present during Patrick's operation, came to visit him. In typical Marty fashion he had taken great care to buy Patrick—a basketball nut—the perfect gift: a statue of a basketball player. But instead of expressing his gratitude for the gift to Marty, Patrick merely groaned, turned over in bed, and showed Marty his back, without saying a single word to him.

As the years went on, Patrick's attitude toward Marty began to soften. Then his antagonism toward Marty flared once more while Patrick lived in our house while I was working in

Australia. One day, Marty wanted to drive Cole, my grandson, to a pinball parlor, but Patrick—who didn't like the way Marty drove—said, "No, I don't want you to drive him." Cole kept on begging for Marty to drive him, but Patrick still refused.

In the end Marty said, "Go fuck yourself and get the hell out of my house!"

So Patrick and his family did.

When I came home from Australia and found them gone, I asked what had happened. Patrick repeated what Marty had said to him, but Marty consistently denied it. I have a feeling that Patrick was telling the truth. Sometimes things come out of Marty's mouth that he doesn't realize he is saying. I think that's what happened in this case.

As time went on, it became obvious that Marty, me, and my children were definitely not destined to ever become the Brady Bunch, or even the Partridge Family, and live happily ever after together. This caused incredible tension between Marty and me, tension that in the end almost destroyed our marriage.

In an attempt to find a solution for the dire situation between us, Marty and I saw a therapist, Ron Podell, who suggested that we separate for a year and, during that time, not talk to each other or see each other. "If, after that, you still feel things are not right between you, then get a divorce" was his advice. For the first three months apart from Marty, I cried every single day. When we split, I moved out of the house, as I was the one who wanted the split. Besides, I knew that Marty would never leave the house. He loved it so much.

I got an apartment in the Valley. Two great gay guys lived on one side of me, and two great lesbians lived on the other. Once I got over the pain of the split from Marty, I had a wonderful time with them.

Then it struck me that until now, I had never lived alone in my entire life. I had always lived with someone. But now I was living alone, and I discovered that I liked it.

Professionally, I was touring the country in my solo concert, and I didn't hear much about Marty, except through the grapevine. I knew he was dating somewhat, but that he had no one special in his life. The same could be said of me.

At the end of our year apart, Ron Podell suggested that Marty and I come to Ron's office and talk about how we each now felt about the other.

I arrived at Ron Podell's office first. Then Marty made his entrance, wearing a big hat and playing the trombone.

"Well, looks like you haven't changed a bit, Marty," I said.

Marty laughed, sat down, and the two of us went through what had happened during our year apart.

Then Ron Podell voiced the $64,000 question: "Do you want to give up on each other? Or do you want to start again?"

We both said that we wanted to start again. Then we left Ron's office hand in hand.

Outside, Marty pushed me up against the car and kissed me and hugged me, and I kissed and hugged him back.

"This is never going to happen to us again," Marty said. And I agreed.

We were back together, and a team once more.

Then tragedy struck again. In November 2003, while I was playing a lawyer in an episode of *Law & Order: Special Victims Unit*, I received a phone call on the set from Sari's son, telling me that she had suddenly died, just the day before. I choked up, and although I tried to carry on with the scene, I was too weak to walk down the stairs to the set, I was so overwhelmed with sorrow.

I am eternally happy that Marty and Shaun are now reconciled and that Patrick and Marty now talk to each other practically every day, they get on so well. And Patrick's two sons adore Marty. They think he is funny and the best thing that ever happened to the human race.

Both Patrick and Ryan now completely understand why I married Marty and the reasons why I have stayed married to him for all these years. They understand totally what we've got together. Now and again they will still say, "Marty, you are crazy, screw you!" But basically they understand—as I do—that Marty is like a child desperate for attention, and that sometimes he will do anything to get it.

Through the years, all my four boys have constantly made me proud and happy. Ryan is a set director and always works extremely hard. Even as a little boy, his room was always picture-perfect, his shoes and clothes put away. He is extremely tidy, just as his father, Jack, always was.

When Ryan was forty-five, he married a beautiful Vietnamese girl, and he had his first child, a daughter, Megan Mae, and we were all thrilled.

Although he is the youngest Cassidy boy, in the last five years, in a strange way, Ryan has emerged as the head of the family. He's the one his brothers call if ever they have a problem. I never expected that to happen, but I am glad.

Of all of Jack's kids, Patrick is the most verbal. He's fun to be around, and his sense of humor resembles Jack's incredibly. Like his father, he's a Broadway star. He's got an amazing voice and has appeared in seven Broadway shows.

For me, the highlight was his 2004 starring role in *42nd Street*, first, because he was brilliant in it, but also because I was starring in the show with him. Which made us the first mother/son ever to appear in the same Broadway show together, an achievement of which I shall always be inordinately proud.

When Patrick first asked me to play Dorothy Brock to his Julian Marsh in *42nd Street*, I wasn't sure that I would be able to do it. After all, I was seventy years old and hadn't appeared in a Broadway show since *Maggie Flynn*, all those years ago, and what a debacle that was!

But Patrick convinced me that I was capable of playing the part of Dorothy Brock and playing it well. When we had our first rehearsal and I really got into the part, he was so impressed by my performance, and so emotional, that tears flowed from him.

So there I was, living in New York and doing nine shows a week for four whole months. Patrick and I lived in the same apartment building, but not in the same apartment, and I loved every minute of living so close to him again and working with him, as well.

Being onstage with Patrick also brought Jack back to me forcefully. Patrick, too, continually evoked his father, asking what Jack would have done at a particular point in the show, how he would have handled a particular song, and how he would have played the part in general.

Doing *42nd Street* with Patrick was a wonderful experience and I wouldn't have missed it for the world.

Patrick is a great performer like his father, and from the time that Patrick was a teenager, he was also the womanizer of the century, just like his father. We clashed bitterly over his wanting to bring girls home with him, so that he could go to bed with them there, in our house.

I put my foot down and told him that no way, under no circumstances, was he allowed to bring a girl home and have sex with her in our house. Like it or not, Patrick had no choice but to accept my decision.

Later on, he invited a beautiful African-American girl to be his prom date. I was cool with that, but then I got a call from her parents saying that they didn't want her to go to the prom with Patrick because it wasn't right. The same thing happened again when Patrick started dating a Jewish girl; her parents called and said that although Patrick was a nice man, he wasn't Jewish, so they didn't want their daughter to date him.

But Patrick did find happiness for a time with the actress Bernadette Peters, who is fourteen years his senior. The age difference didn't trouble Patrick, or me. I admired Bernadette, and so did Patrick. She is a wonderful woman, and they had a wonderful time together.

Nowadays, Patrick is doing well in his career, and today he produces shows more often than he appears in them, and fortunately, his private life, too, is a great success. He is married to a beautiful choreographer, and together they have two marvelous sons.

As for David, I've always considered him my fourth son, and he's always treated me with great kindness and courtesy. When we first met, his mother had painted me as a scarlet lady and a wicked stepmother, but as David sweetly said of me years later, "I wanted to hate her, but in minutes warmed to her." The feeling was mutual.

David is nine years older than Shaun, eleven years older than Patrick and fifteen years older than Ryan. At first, David was afraid that he would be an outsider among my three sons and me, but when he and I started making *The Partridge Family* together, David grew closer and closer to me and the boys.

He was a sensitive and perceptive boy, and after Jack's death, I was surprised to learn that he had been aware of how I had always put Jack up on a pedestal and deferred to him and his wishes, even after I had become a star in Hollywood, and Jack had not.

"She was the star, but my father was the maestro," David characterized it later. "She lived for Jack Cassidy."

Through the years, it's been clear to me that David is extremely like Jack. David has his charm, and also his dark side, which led to his battle with drugs, about which he has written so movingly in his book *Could It Be Forever?: My Story.*

He wasn't good at school, and if you read his book, it is easy to understand why. He confesses that he started taking drugs when he was twelve years old. From cocaine to everything else. Jack and I both knew that he was doing drugs. We just weren't sure what.

At the height of David's fame and fortune, he did have a big ego for a time, but he was young and handsome and his success inevitably went to his head. David has had three marriages, and my happiest memory of him is when he married his current wife, Sue, the mother of his son, Beau. David also has a daughter, Katy, by a previous relationship. She is an accomplished actress.

Marrying Sue and having Beau grounded David. She was a songwriter, a performer, and she adored David. And I was glad that he found her. Beau is twenty-one and is talented and has his own band, called Beau Cassidy and the Sundance Kid. A great name.

Professionally, David is still in great demand and has dates all over the country, in particular in casinos.

He is still close to his brothers. Last Mother's Day, he left a sweet message on my answering machine:

"Dearest Shirley, I wish you a wonderful Mother's Day and just to tell you that you have been a major part of my life and a major part of my career.

"You have been such a wonderful mother to me. You have helped me in so many ways. I admire you so much and I am so grateful to have had you in my life, and to have you in my life now. And there's not a day that goes by without me thinking of something that you once said to me. Thank you, Shirley."

In 1995, Shaun did Willy Russell's *Blood Brothers* with David on Broadway. Shaun and David were playing fraternal twins who had been separated at birth, and David was thrilled that Shaun joined him in the play. Ever since I'd first met David, I was always aware that he had a good heart, and he loved working with Shaun, as Shaun has always been so down-to-earth. Eventually, though, Shaun gave up the theater in favor of creating, writing, and producing shows himself.

In *2001*, I actually appeared in one of them, *Cover Me: Based on the True Life of an FBI Family*, in which I played the mother of a murderer. It was a good part, but Shaun was a tough director, and when I flubbed my lines for some reason, he was most scathing, and rightly so!

In July 2009, Shaun directed Patrick and David in the TV sitcom *Ruby & the Rockits*. Patrick played Patrick Gallagher, who was taking care of Ruby, the daughter of his rock-star brother, David Gallagher. Although the show pulled a 1.8 million audience in the season premiere, it was shut down after a year. However, today Shaun remains a well-respected writer and producer, and I am proud of him and his brothers, who are all wonderful to me and caring.

I love how they are all so close to one another.

FIFTEEN

Walking On

One of the happiest memories of my career (note: *career,* not *life*) was appearing in the TV movie *Hidden Places*, in 2006, for which I won an Emmy nomination, as I was playing Aunt Batty, against type.

In 2006, too, I was offered a movie part a million miles removed from Laurey, Julie, or Marian the librarian: the part of Grace in the movie *Grandma's Boy*.

My agent sent me the script, saying that the producer, Adam Sandler, and the director, Nicholaus Goossen, wanted me to pick which of the old ladies I'd like to play.

Well, the biggest role was Mama (which Doris Roberts ended up playing), but my heart was set on playing the geriatric sex bomb, Grace. The script was funny, vulgar, and I adored it.

Making the movie was fun from morning to night. In one scene us old ladies get high on marijuana, which we thought was sugar. And in another, I am half-naked and rolling around in bed with Nick Swardson, who was born in 1976!

My love scene with Nick, who also co-wrote the movie, was hysterical. Despite our vast age difference, I tell him that the moment I met him, I had my eye on him and knew instantly that he was the one for me. Consequently, I won't let him alone, and in the end we do go to bed together. Along the way, I tell him that I once gave Charlie Chaplin a hand job, and chances are he's never even heard of Charlie.

After we've had sex, he turns around and tells me, "You were my first."

I answer, "You were my three thousand two hundred and twenty-third."

The movie was really funny, and to this day teenage guys come up to me and, with a twinkle in their eyes, say, "I just loved you in *Grandma's Boy*!"

Quite recently, I was sitting in an airport lounge when an old lady hobbled up to me. "I loved you in . . ."

I expected her to say *Oklahoma!* or *Carousel* or *The Music Man*.

"I loved you in *Grandma's Boy*," she finally said. She was around ninety-six years old.

I loved playing a sexy old lady in *Grandma's Boy*, not just because the movie was hysterically funny, but because I've always believed that old age and sexuality are not incompatible. And that a woman can retain her sexuality at any age.

Marty agrees with me and, in 2009, convinced *Playboy* boss Hugh Hefner that it was time that an older woman displayed her charms in the pages of his magazine.

So Hefner agreed to make me his latest center-fold and invited me up to his mansion for a photo shoot.

When I got there, I was presented with an array of beautiful see-through negligees, but from the first, I made it clear that although I was happy to expose my legs, that would be it.

Everyone present agreed that would be fine.

So they made me up, and I spent all day at the mansion. We selected a flimsy, blue negligee, and I posed all over the Playboy Mansion, leaning against doorways, and lying across a glamorous king-size bed, revealing my legs and looking as fetching as possible.

Afterward, Hefner examined the pictures with his eagle eye and pronounced, "Shirley is lovely, and the pictures are lovely, but I want more nudity."

Sadly, I had shown the camera all of my body that I was willing to show. "That kind of nudity isn't right for me anymore," I had to admit, and the subject was closed.

I wasn't prepared to bare all for *Playboy*, but I still want to make it clear that I believe that a woman can remain sexual right through her seventies and eighties and beyond. I am living proof of that.

In 1990, I had one ovary and my uterus removed because I had a big tumor there, which luckily was not cancerous. Fortunately this hasn't affected my sexuality at all.

I've always been an extremely sexual woman, easily aroused, and intensely orgasmic. Despite my advanced years, that hasn't changed a bit, although it can take longer than before for me to achieve sexual fulfillment these days. And it's often easier for me to achieve it through masturbation and not during intercourse or oral sex.

As I recounted before, Jack initiated me into sex and I had my first orgasm with him, and it was wonderful. Afterward he said, "Whenever you are alone, and you think of me, this is what you can do: you can masturbate."

Jack was my sexual Svengali. He taught me everything about sex, and he taught me how to masturbate and never to be ashamed about doing it. He would watch me masturbating, and I would love it and never be shy or inhibited in any way.

I'm still the same. And I still masturbate. I don't romanticize what I am doing. I don't have a bubble bath beforehand or turn out the lights or play sensual music. I just use Vaseline and a finger. And my fantasies.

Although in my movies I've kissed some of the world's most sexy men—Marlon Brando, Frank Sinatra, Jimmy Stewart, Rod Steiger, and more—

and in my private life was married to sex God Jack Cassidy, I never think of any real-life men when I fantasize during masturbation. Instead, I get aroused by imagining a faceless, macho guy.

And while I'm masturbating, I say his dialogue and mine, out loud. If people heard the explicit words I say, they would be shocked. I love words, and I talk the fantasy through. I don't need satin sheets or French perfume to get sexually excited. Basically, the more I talk the fantasy through, the more aroused I get, and the stronger my orgasms end up being. I can have one or two a session, and I love each and every one of them.

I need to have an orgasm every now and again for the release and the pleasurable feeling it creates in me. Masturbation, you see, is great for relaxation, great for the skin, and a wonderful way of feeling and remaining young, I firmly believe.

I'm not the only woman of my age to believe that masturbation is important for our well-being. I have female friends of my age who also love to pleasure themselves. After all, although our bodies may be old and wrinkled, our desires can still remain fresh and young.

When we older women masturbate, at least we don't have to dress up or apply makeup or worry that we look our age. When we masturbate, we don't have to put on airs and graces, but can just be ourselves and enjoy ourselves and feel alive and renewed.

Marty and I still have sex, but he is also aware that I masturbate, and it doesn't bother him at all. The other morning, I came down to breakfast and told him that I'd masturbated the night before, but that it hadn't gone well.

"What did you do wrong?" he cracked.

Sometimes it simply isn't the right time and my mind just isn't tuned in on sex.

I do think a woman should take care of her body however old she is. If you don't like your body, go to the gym and work at it. I spend an hour a day there, and I always watch what I eat and eat much less meat than I used to.

In 1984, the *National Enquirer* claimed that Marty had driven me to drink and that I had a problem with alcohol. They photographed me at a party with wineglasses everywhere, but they didn't all belong to me. Marty and I sued and beat the *Enquirer* and their claims were retracted. Nowadays, I have a martini every afternoon at five, but other than that, I never indulge in alcohol.

Luckily, Marty thinks I've still got a beautiful body, even though it is old, and every now and again I take all my clothes off in front of him and shake my tits at him, and he loves it.

I love dressing up in glamorous clothes for him, but I'm not one for makeup and I don't dye my hair. I use a special skin-care product, but my mother always had beautiful skin and at the age of sixty-eight didn't have a single wrinkle on her face, and fortunately, I think it is genetic.

Sadly, when my mother was in her late sixties, she was in a wheelchair because she had arthritis, and so did both my aunts. I have inherited the disease, and my body is filled with arthritis. I had a knee replacement and will eventually need to have the other one replaced as well.

Marty and I generally live a quiet life in our stone-and-wood, country-style house in Encino, along with our golden retriever, King, and our Welsh corgi, Hannah. Marty is a hoarder, so every room is filled with his papers, his photographs, his show-business memorabilia. The lovely thing about the house, though, is that it has an upstairs floor, where he usually stores everything he wants to keep long-term.

And even if he doesn't, the house covers five thousand square feet, has five bedrooms, five bathrooms, a playroom for the children, and a movie theater, so there is plenty of space for us both, and we are extremely happy there.

One of my great joys is our house in Fawnskin, on the other side of Bear Lake. Fawnskin is an hour-and-a-half drive from Los Angeles, in the San Bernardino Mountains. Fawnskin used to be an artists' colony, is 6,827 feet above sea level, and has a population of just three hundred people, which appeals to my small-town mentality.

I'd always wanted a house in the mountains as I've always been a big skier. So in 1976, I decided I needed more solitude and to luxuriate in my love for nature and the countryside, and to ski. I went up to Bear Lake and consulted a Realtor there. She wanted to show me houses on Bear Lake itself, but I didn't want to live right on the lake. Instead, I wanted to live somewhere more isolated, away from people and crowds. And Fawnskin fit the bill perfectly.

She took me up a little dirt road in Fawnskin, with coyotes frolicking in the undergrowth, and showed me this wooden house with a terrace looking out on a vista that feels as if you were standing on a mountaintop in Switzerland and gazing down at the most beautiful view in the world, a view to die for.

I didn't even go inside the house. I bought it then and there, paying $62,000 for the two-bedroom house and garage on six acres. The house came furnished, with a piano. I redid the whole thing, then bought nine more acres and converted the garage into a guesthouse.

One of my greatest pleasures in life nowadays is to sit on the deck of the main house, my 5:00 p.m. martini in one hand and a box of chocolates in the other, and talk to the coyotes.

Eleven years ago, Marty and I were in Fawnskin. The town is small, with just a tiny market, a tiny deli, plus a Moose lodge. We had lunch at the North Shore Café and noticed a FOR SALE sign on a stretch of land across the street, right next to the Moose lodge.

"I just hope they don't build a 7-Eleven on it," I said to Marty. Within hours, he checked the price of the land, we got a great deal, and we bought it on the spot. The date was September 10, 2001. The very next day, 9/11 exploded on the world.

When the news broke, Marty and I had exactly the same thought: to create a park on our newly acquired land as a tribute to all those who lost their lives in the tragedy of 9/11.

It all started with our getting a girder from the ruins of the Twin Towers and putting it in the center of our park. Fawn Memorial Park, we called it. On the walls around the park are pictures and statues of the brave firemen and policemen who were killed that day, with a small stage in the middle of it. Some wonderful people helped us with the funding to get the park going, but we still have financial difficulties in maintaining it.

To aid in that, and because I love it, I continue to work as much as possible. I would love to do another TV series or a movie. And if I do, I hope I will be cast against type once more, as I was in *Elmer Gantry* and in *Grandma's Boy*. Almost half a century divides those two roles, but I loved playing both of them, primarily because I have always liked to shock people a bit. Despite my age, I still do.

317

I am now seventy-nine years old, and although I can't believe it, life is still good. I have four sons (I always view David as mine) and twelve grandchildren, and Marty and I have a close and loving marriage.

Now and again, though, the thought has run through my mind about both the men I married —about Jack and about Marty—that I am not altogether sure if they married little Shirley Mae Jones or Shirley Jones the movie star. I guess I'll never really know.

The main thing is that today I am so thankful that I have a partner I can cry with, laugh with, and who is always there for me. Marty takes good care of me, makes sure all the bills are paid on time, and is thrilled about everything that I do professionally and is glad to be part of it.

Every night as I sit on a chair, sipping my martini, Marty sits on the couch opposite me, and we have conversations about everybody and everything in our lives, and it's great. We talk about family, friends, and business projects. Marty tells me jokes and makes me laugh continuously.

I love that we share everything, even though we are so very different. Yet we are still together, we still love each other, and whatever anybody else thinks of Marty and of our marriage, I know the truth: I have found my ultimate Prince Charming and I'm living happily ever after with him.

ACKNOWLEDGMENTS

All my thanks to the great team at Gallery:

Mitchell Ivers (Senior Editor)

Jen Bergstrom (Vice President and Publisher)

Louise Burke (President and Publisher)

Jen Robinson (Vice President, Publicity Director)

Natasha Simons (Editorial Assistant)

John Paul Jones
       (Associate Director of Copyediting)

Lisa Litwack (Art Director)

Thanks to my agent, Dan Strone, CEO at Trident Media Group, and a true facilitator, and to his assistant, Kseniya Zaslavskaya.

Thanks to Rick Hersh, who introduced me to Dan in the first place.

And thanks to Wendy Leigh, irrepressible co-writer extraordinaire, without whom I'd still be staring at an empty typewriter.

Center Point Large Print
600 Brooks Road / PO Box 1
Thorndike ME 04986-0001 USA

(207) 568-3717

US & Canada:
1 800 929-9108
www.centerpointlargeprint.com